Blessings!

# Passionate Endorsements from Readers

"Heavenletters never fail to open my heart and let divine light and love shine in. And what a sweet, healing blessing that is!"
*Cindy Buck, Co-author,* Chicken Soup for the Gardener's Soul

"Extraordinary book! Exactly what the world needs to hear right now. Everyone can hear the Voice of God, we are all born with the ability. This book is absolutely phenomenal!"
*Katharine Giovanni, Author,* God, is that you?

"*A Course in Miracles* states that the Voice for God will speak directly to us. *Heavenletters* fulfills that promise."
*Dr. Mawiyah Clayborne, Author,* How to Remember Your Bliss

"If you have ever wished that God would simply send you a letter and answer all your questions – and who hasn't – then reading Heavenletters is a must. Every letter arrives wrapped in Love and is delivered straight to your heart. Savor each letter as it enlightens, inspires, encourages, calms and delights. Your letters and answers have arrived, all you have to do is read them and let them work their magic in your life."
*Beca Lewis, Author,* Living in Grace: The Shift to Spiritual Perception

"The vibration of love, compassion, hope, joy, forgiveness, and Oneness literally jumps into my heart during and after reading Heavenletters."
*Allan Silberhartz, Producer,* Bridging Heaven and Earth TV Show

"I know in this age many wonder if God exists, even less worry about talking to God. Yet we know that one of the enduring dynamics of almost every world religion is our relationship to the Divine. At bottom, most of us yearn to be mystics, while at the same time are afraid. The Society of Friends (Quakers) have long held that a direct experience of the Divine is the heart of faith. To those who remain skeptical today in a world torn apart by religious wars, I would simply say: Read some Heaven Letters, for there you will encounter a dialog between the human and Divine like few others you have read in our time."

*Rev. Dr. John C. Morgan, Author,* Awakening the Soul

"I have been resistant to the sweet way God is presented in Heavenletters because there is so much suffering in the world. But about ¾ thru a letter, I became a bit overwhelmed with some joy...a presence of...well...God maybe...something soft and that 'experience' I tend to call spiritual. Wow. The mind is such an enemy when it comes to 'knowing God.' I love God with all I am, and I know you do. All weirdness and questions disappear when the mind stops."

*Rudy Wilson, Author,* The Red Truck

"My housemate and I have been studying consciousness for some time, but nothing so profound as Heavenletters has reached into our hearts and reconciled our minds. Pure truth through and through. Love speaking as truth. WOW! Words cannot describe the feelings evoked by these thoughts of GOD. We are left with stillness in our minds and love beating in our hearts."

*Peter Slane,* D.C., N.D.

"My heart has been soaring ever since I made the connection with Heavenletters. It isn't just the words – it's the Love energies that come from them."

*Joyce Zakrajsek, Astrologer* www.astronumeropsychic.com

# Heavenletters

## Love Letters from God

## Book One

# Gloria Wendroff

1st WORLD
LIBRARY
Literary Society

# HEAVENLETTERS
## LOVE LETTERS FROM GOD
### BOOK ONE

## Gloria Wendroff

© The Godwriting International Society of Heaven Ministries 2004

Published by 1stWorld Library
1100 North 4th St. Suite 131, Fairfield, Iowa 52556
TEL: 641-209-5000 • FAX: 641-209-3001 • WEB: www.1stworldlibrary.net

First Edition

LCCN: 2004092813

ISBN: 1-59540-989-0

Cover Design George Foster www.Fostercovers.com

Readers are invited to contact www.1stworldlibrary.net for information on services provided by 1stWorld Library Publishing Exchange:

- Editing
- Layout
- Formatting
- Cover design
- Marketing

- Library of Congress
- ISBN numbers
- Bar codes
- Media contacts
- Book signings

# Table of Contents

# 91 Heavenletters

# Introduction

Hello, I'm Dr. Bernie Siegel, and it is my privilege to introduce you to a series of messages from God called
Heavenletters™.

Some of you may be familiar with my work and books, the
most well-known being *Love, Medicine & Miracles*, and the most
recent, but not the last, *How to Heal*.

We are all pieces of the puzzle of creation, and every single
one of us is needed for its completion. Considering what the
world is like after all these years, it's obviously not easy to
solve the puzzle. But with God's help, I think we can understand and solve it with love.

It strikes me as absurd that the word *God* is removed from
anything. I like that Gloria calls God *God* outright and, furthermore, that God speaks to us right now.

I do not picture God as a person sitting somewhere direct-
ing traffic! In truth, God is indefinable. God's wisdom, however, is available to us all. The great sages tell us that we can
hear the Word of God. The Kabbalah talks exactly about what
Heavenletters are doing

Catherine of Siena, in the fourteenth century, presented a
series of questions to God and received responses and

amplifications. She called these dialogs "the bridge." Her intimate conversations with God have been published in a book called *The Dialogue.*

Catherine said she knew it was God because of the beneficial effects of the dialog.

I sometimes wonder if Gloria wasn't Catherine in a past life.

If I had to attempt to define the Indefinable, I would say God is loving, intelligent, conscious Energy.

Heavenletters works on the level of consciousness and heart-wisdom, not intellect and head-wisdom.

As studies are showing, the heart contains nerve cells very similar to the brain and endocrine cells. The heart is more than a pump, believe me. I am speaking as a physician and scientist.

The heart is the cord that binds together the spiritual and the physical, the soul, and the finite world. Heavenletters is like that cord.

When we hear God's words, we bring energy, consciousness, and love and light to ourselves and others. God's light never ceases to exist, and we are all luminaries like the stars, immortal and lighting the darkness for others to find their way, just as the stars guided the early explorers.

An ancient rabbi said that man was created so that he might lift up the Heavens. Why not? Who knows what we are capable of giving and doing.

One day our love will include all of mankind, and we will live the Oneness of God. One day, not God willing, but man willing, it will be on earth as it is in Heaven, and there will be peace on earth and good will to men.

You are about to embark on an adventure with God. You are the hero. Listen well. I will leave you to your journey, for each must go on his or her own journey to find one's treasure chest.

So now, with God's blessing, find the treasure and return with it to the benefit of all.

Peace be with you, and as John Lennon wrote: "Imagine all the people living for today. You may say I'm a dreamer, but I'm not the only one. I hope someday you'll join us, and the world will live as One."

Bernie S. Siegel, M.D.<br>
Woodbridge, Connecticut

# Author's Preface

I am excited to introduce you to these beautiful messages from God. I say God. Some of you might prefer to say Higher Self or Divine Consciousness or Spirit. No matter. We mean the same.

How did it happen that I started to hear and write down what God said?

My first answer is I don't really know.

My second answer is it came from every thread of my life.

And the third answer is it doesn't matter. What God says matters!

But I do know this: Heavenletters didn't come from a flash of lightning. It was not an enormous event.

In loneliness and wanting and wondering and doubting and ignorance, I asked my human questions, and answers came, and the Answerer said Yes, He was God.

But how could these words from my pen be His? I knew they weren't mine, but how could God's words come and come to me? Oh, how I wanted confirmation. So, innocently, to anyone who asked me what I was doing those days, I said: "Oh, I'm writing down God's words now in a notebook and..."

I didn't get confirmation. I got funny looks. So I kept God's messages to myself for about a year until I cared more of what God had to say than what others thought. Heaven had to be extended, and I had to extend it. So bravely I emailed daily Heavenletters to a friend or two, and then there were eight. And then there were sixteen. And then readers became subscribers, and then sixteen became sixty and so on, and Heavenletters arose.

As God listened to us and we listened to God, it became a possibility that He did indeed love us, as is, each one of us personally as well as collectively. This possibility grew to be our experience. We might doubt ourselves again and again, but the practicality of God as an intimate Companion of our hearts continued to grow. Little by little, our acceptance that God knew us and that we knew God grew into the beginnings of faith.

And so God would charm our lives and change them.

You can pick up God's love and wisdom now as it is placed here before you. This is where you come in! You who are reading God's words are meant to read them. They are for you. God gave them to you. With God's blessings, you enter Heaven now.

# A Note about Gender

Before you begin, I'd like to say a few words about gender and capitalization as they appear in Heavenletters™.

You will see that God is referred to as He. Of course, this is not meant to limit anyone's conception of God.

Here is what God Himself says:

"I am the God the Father and God the Mother. But I am neither male nor female, and I am both. I am All. Male and female are energies. He and She are manners of speaking. All words are metaphors for the energy they represent.

"If you call to Me as Mother Divine, I bear that in mind in My answer. But it is you who calls Me Mother Divine or Father God.

"I am I, no matter what form you like Me to be in. How you address Me is up to you. It doesn't matter to Me. You matter to Me, and I will respond to your heart."

# A Note about Capitalization

As for the extended use of capital letters, I am partial to them! I especially like to capitalize Sun and Light when they represent God. My proofreaders tell me there are some inconsistencies. I hope you won't mind.

In one case, however, unusual capitalization was definitely God's choice, as follows:

"All My children are God Beings. Only, on earth you are called human beings. Uncapitalized is how you are described, and lower case is how you have thought of yourself. I would have you think of yourself as Human Beings, for I would have you think more highly of yourself.

"If it were up to Me, I would call you God Beings, for you are Beings of God."

[*If you would like to know more about the Story of Heavenletters, please visit* http://www.heavenletters.org/storyofhl.html]

# Dedication

To my dear mother and father
who worked so hard,
had so little,
and gave so much.
Thank you.

# Acknowledgments

To my beloved daughter Lauren who supported Heavenletters™ financially and in every way. She helped with every decision, came to the rescue when there were computer problems, and was always thinking of ways to make me happy.

To Bernie Siegel who answered my email and became a mentor and friend, totally dedicated in devotion to God and peace and kindness to all.

To Allan Silberhartz, who kept me on the straight and narrow, calling me often, helping me to focus and get the book together, making me laugh and listen to his delightful brand of common sense.

To Rodney Charles, well-named the Patron Saint of Spiritual Writers, who helped me to believe in myself.

To Tony Ellis, supreme editor, who sees the infinite and the finite, and has a knack of making me amenable to change.

To Margaret Yoder Weiner and Tracey Bennett, master proofreaders, who proofread God's words with full hearts and impeccable skill and granted me poetic license.

To Carolyn Agner who so graciously and magnificently manages Heaven's web site before she goes to work in the morning as if it were the easiest thing in the world.

To Annette Bradley who saw the need, stepped in, and archives Heavenletters year after year.

To all those precious souls who so graciously volunteer their hearts and time to Heavenletters, to the beautiful subscribers who love God's words and don't mind saying so, and to the amazing Godwriters™ whose own Godwriting™ inspires me every time.

To all the teachers who have inspired me, from Miss Bancroft, my second-grade teacher, and up, including the great writers and sages, past and present, who fill my heart with gratitude.

And, above all, I thank God for His eternal love and wisdom and blessings and for the vastness of His joy He so generously shares with us all and for miraculously calling on me to be His 'typewriter'.

# God's Introduction

The heart of what I give you in these messages is not the message itself. What you extract from My letters may be succinct and wonderful, but it is only a thimbleful of what I give you. I pour down love upon you and a certain lyric wisdom far more than any words you extract.

My messages here are far more than their message. Messages are not enough. Knowing all the messages in the world is not enough. The message I give you is more than any synopsis of it. What I give you cannot be defined. The heart of My messages cannot be contained in words. The words are peripheral to My heart. There is nothing for you to learn here but to be with Me.

Would you not sit down with Me? We do not have to speak, or We can engage in idle chatter, or We can talk in circles, or We can hit the nail on the head. What does it matter? It matters that We sit together.

We are together for the engagement of Ourselves. We sit and hold hands. That is enough. A few moments with Me goes a long way. You do not necessarily know what you take away from Our meeting.

Be My love, won't you?

What is My message here for you today? Forget about it. Just be with Me, and allow Me to take you places. Do not sit up so straight. Do not take notes. Just rest in Me.

Let Me tug at your heart. Let Me weave whatever I weave. Let Me pat your brow. Let Me pull worry lines away. Let Me enjoy these few moments with you. What are you in a rush to learn? What must you complete so soon? Just abide with Me.

Give Me your heart, not your mind. There is enough mind in the world and perhaps not enough heart. In any case, I ask for your heart. I wish to entwine it with Mine. Let Our hearts rub elbows. Sit down with Me a while.

# 1
# Open your heart like beating wings

The ship you ride on is My heart. Think of it.

Giants walk the earth, and they are you. You are greatness encapsulated into a Human form. Find out Who you are. See bigger. Do not accept the limits of your form. That is what you have been doing. No longer accept limits. Unlimit yourself. I put no limits on you. I never did, and I don't now. What limit do you think that the Limitless can put?

Cease believing in limits. There are none but those in which you believe. Your heart can travel anywhere. Your heart can take you everywhere. Your heart expands your mind. Your mind accepts limits. Your heart knows better. In your heart of hearts, you know the vastness of this enterprise of life that you have set forth on.

Remove your clinging to limits as you would a vine that has wrapped itself around you. Cling now to the vastness of no limits.

Nothing limits you. Do you hear this? Nothing limits you.

Adherence to old ways blocks your view. Look to greatness and not selfishness. Look to Me and you will abandon smallness. Selfishness is nothing but small vision. You haven't been seeing far enough. You haven't really seen what is right in front of you either.

Be a sighted Human Being. Eat the loaf of life. Know what you have been given. Accept what you have been given. You have been given everything. And you have accepted a small crust of it. That is rude rather than grateful.

Grateful isn't an emotion. It is a seeing. See that which you have been given and then you will be magnanimous. Gratitude is seeing the treasures heaped upon you. Ingratitude is not seeing.

The change to make today is in your seeing. Then you can begin your life as it was given to you.

Splendid, splendid are your opportunities. You have been given a grant from Heaven. How will you use it? This is the question. How do you want to use it? I will tell you.

You want to use it vastly. You do not want confines of anything. Open your heart like beating wings, and see where it takes you. It takes you to Me, and that is gratitude in the life you have been granted. Take wing on gratitude.

Gratitude is awareness. If you do not see the food, how will you eat? See the table set before you, and avail yourself of it.

You are My gift. I have given you. I haven't given you for nothing. I have given you for something, and that something is Greatness. Accept the possibility of what I say. I say you are My magnificence. Accept the title I give you. The title I give you is your Identity. Accept no other.

You live in a world bigger than you knew. You are not held to time and space. You are held to Great Love.

Be that which you are.

I name you Love. I appoint you Love. I appoint you Mine. And I set you forth to till the field. Till hearts. Till your own. Accept the title I give you. Accept, Child of God.

## 2

# What if you are a light that lights hearts?

Like the Sun and the Moon, I have followed you and bestowed upon you all manner of light. You thought you were walking in a wilderness, and now you discover that you have been walking in Paradise with a God Who loves you, a God Who created the moisture of the grape and the winding of its vine, a God Who created the pointedness of a pine tree and the shade of an elm, and put you under both. I spilled out all kinds of treasure before you. I spilled it all out, the seas and the land, the sand and the grape, the mountain and the vale.

I spilled out My love in every form imaginable. Did I leave out anything? What combination have I not made? And I made you and gave you the whole universe to play with.

Here you are, under a Christmas tree, laden with so many gifts you don't know what is before you and what to open first.

From where did the gifts come? Who is the Giver? And who receives? Who exchanges gifts with Me? Who gives Me his joy? Who appreciates the treasures put before him? Who is in awe of the life I have given him? Who knows that he has been enriched?

Be children who receive. Receive, and you can appreciate.

First you have to receive. First you have to see the gifts poured upon you. Then you can open them. Then you can see what you have been given.

Perhaps one gift is behind another, and at first, you don't see it. You bemoan: "Where is my gift? Why haven't I been given it? I haven't been given the one thing I really want." And you search. And each gift you open isn't quite yet what you wanted, or you tire of it before it is hardly unwrapped.

You live in a treasure-chest, and you think you have been denied. You think something has been withheld from you. But you have been the withholder. You have withheld yourself from horizons before you. Reach out your eyes and absorb.

Desire that you appreciate Creation. Desire that you begin to see and appreciate the wonders before you. Desire to see the unopened packages waiting for you, wanting you as much as you want them.

What does life hold for you? Do you see the upward spiral? Start following the spiral up with your eyes. You will be surprised with what you see. And what you see you can give.

Abundance lies before you. Abundance lies within you. You can be generous, for One has been generous with you.

When you think you have been denied, you hold back. Deny yourself denial, and know you have treasure heaped before you. Nothing has been denied you. Everything has been given you.

What if you knew you had been given everything, how different would your life be? When you set out on a journey with everything you need, how do you feel? You have all the resources of the entire universe at your feet. And you are surrounded by all of Heaven.

Furthermore, what if you knew you were royalty? What

then? The same *you* who walks down the street walks diffe-rently. The same *you* who sees sees differently. The same *you* who speaks speaks differently. Accept your inheritance now.

What if you are a light that lights the hearts of man?

I say you are. I say you are a beacon light on earth. I say that when you recognize and acknowledge your light, you will see more and further and you will be in awe before My benefi-cence. Be in awe now.

You walk through a land filled with treasure, and you only have to look, and appreciation comes of itself. Appreciate the gifts and the Appreciator of All. Appreciate what you have been given and hold your light high so that others may also see what they have been given.

## 3

# Deep within its beat, your heart made an oath to look for Me

Have the faith in Me that I deserve. If you cannot have faith in Me for your sake, then have faith in Me for My sake.

Fulfill My faith in you. I reach My hand out to you, and I ask you to put your hand in Mine. You say that you don't see My hand; you say you don't know where it is. All the while, My hand reaches for yours. And all the while you grope. My children, there is no other hand.

It is true there are angel souls on earth, and they will give you a hand up, and so you have ladders on earth. But that is the trial offer, the one that is sent to you in the mail. It is a small per cent of the Total Offer. Send for more. Send in your order for the Golden Ladder of Truth that awaits you.

There is no price assigned to it. The price is to ask. That is all. The price is to reach out and up. The price is to return the stamped self-addressed order card. The price is to place your order.

I have told you before that you do not ask for enough. I do not mean number of requests. You have plenty of those, but they miss the point.

I mean the one request, the one you dilly-dally about, the

one request that your awareness be utterly joined with Mine. That is all that is lacking. Your awareness. Surely Mine is not. We are already joined.

What a difference when your awareness of Our Unity joins with My Awareness. How far we travel when you realize Our Oneness. That is Self-Realization.

If all is Oneness, then there is One Self for you to realize. You have searched for your identity in small places. Now look for your Universal Identity. Look for your place in the stars. Enough looking at your feet. Look to where the Light comes from. Oh, My Beloveds, how I yearn for you to see Me.

To see Me, see with your heart. Your heart has eyes that see. Consider your heart a sense far greater than the others you count on. Use the one sense that resides in your heart, or you have no sense at all.

The physical senses are feelers that touch your environment and bring it to your heart. The five senses are a prelude to your heart. Their information goes to your heart, and it is adjudicated there in the bank of your heart. The adjudication of your heart is not judgment but rather a filter that separates the dross from the gold.

Deep within its beat, your heart has made an oath to look for Me and to find Me. I am Truth. Obey the oath your heart made long ago.

Your heart of hearts knows that it never lost Me. It knows I reign. It knows that you make My heart complete. It knows that We feel a mutual yearning. It is the same yearning, yours for Me, Mine for you. The only difference is that I know you will answer, but you do not have the faith that I will.

It is a simple thing to answer My call for you. It is I Who has a calling. You have an answering. All you can do is join in on My calling. I call you. Answer Me.

You wait for an answer from Me. Hear My call to you. I await your answer. Choose to recognize Our connection. Choose to know it. Choose to bare your heart to it. I enter through your heart, and I stay there. Put your awareness on Our Union in your heart. Open Our connection to the universe. Reveal Me to yourself.

# Heavenletters, Love Letters from God

## Book One

"You create the world as you walk through it."

Heavenletters, Love Letters from God, Book One, p.26

gloria@heavenletters.org

www.heavenletters.org

641-472-4529

# 4

# You are a bird of God that has nothing to do but sing His Greatness

Today you are God's pure spirit, unladen of the past. You wake unsullied. You wake up to Me.

It is I Who wakes you. The tide of God wakes you just like the Moon pulls the seas. I pull you to Me. "Awake, awake," I say. And you push off the covers of the past, and you know that you awaken to Me and not to thoughts of the past.

For one moment you awake to the sense of Oneness with Me rather than with aches of regret of what is done or undone or despair for what is yet to be done or occur.

Regret and despair are of the same. Regret looks back, and despair looks ahead. Our sense of Oneness is not a hold-over nor a lingerer, though you can enjoy this awareness forever.

Remember, awareness is not a thought. You have a nose, but you are not always thinking, "I have a nose."

You have a God, ever-present, all-seeing, All-Being. You always have Me. Your awareness of Me is like lowering your weary body into a tub of warm water. It is like getting out of the bath to a large warmed towel. It is like the pouring of scented oils on your skin. It is like getting dressed in silk. It is like going into the fresh air and breathing it. It is like a breeze so fair passing your cheek that you are left in wonder. It is like your eyes sighting the ribbons of dawn. It is like an Ah of a song beginning that arises from your willing throat and encompasses the whole of the universe like the Sun itself.

One note of Oneness issues forth from your throat as though you are a bird of God that has nothing to do but sing His Greatness. And this bird of God sings God's song to himself and to all who can hear.

Awareness of Me is an understanding. It is a basis. It is an acceptance of the God content of your life. It is an acceptance of your own aura, for it is My light that shines in and around you. Let your aura be greater. Accept the light I give you. It is 360-degree light. It lights beneath, beside, and above. It merges with the Light above, and so My light and your own light shine on you. You bask in the Light of God. You are never without it. You carry your own Sun within you. You are a satellite to the Sun. You are a sun who shines to the Sun.

He Who gave you breath takes your breath away in the exquisiteness of your awareness of Him and His creation. You breathe deep of the breathlessness of your awe. Your cozy awe is a continuation of the Ah your singing throat sang out at the dawning of your awareness.

And I sing My song to you. I never stopped. You pick up My one note, and it issues forth from your throat. You sing My song that you hear. Never let Me out of your hearing. Don't let Me out of your sight. Touch My heart. Taste My love. Breathe the scent of Me and stop wondering where it comes from. It is enough to know that all beauty comes from Me.

Your earthly senses are like five streams that meet in an ocean. The five streams stream from God and stream back to Him. It is a loop, this God almost-experience.

You cannot experience God as you experience a baseball game. You cannot experience Me as you do a feast at the table.

But you can experience Me as the glow in your eyes that watches the game and devours the feast. I see into your eyes, and I see from them. We are the loop of love that winds infinitely and finds itself.

# 5

# Who owns a river? Or the ocean?

Often you have thought of Me as One Who takes away from you. Undo that thinking, and you will see eminent change in your life.

What you see as taken away from you are leaves on the tree that fall in autumn. It is a slipping into another realm and other possibilities and ways of loving. When your body ceases – something you half pray for and half resent – you enter another dimension. You are not dismantled. Only your attachment is removed from you.

Attachment is your struggle. It is easy for you to care but hard to care without attachment. Attachment is adding possessions onto you. But there are no possessions. There is only a stream you mill through.

Who owns a river? Or the ocean? All an idea, this idea of ownership. The ocean is Mine.

When you walk through a beautiful forest, you enjoy it, and your heart is lifted in your passing through. A forest is My gift to you, and you walk through it. It is given to you, not to possess, but to walk through.

When you believe you own the forest, you start to see the forest as something that can be taken from you. You stop seeing it as a beautiful passage.

Your walk through it becomes more like a supervisorship and you become fraught with worry which is a name for your fear of loss.

Not only is what you like to possess not owned by you, it is not possessable. Belongings do not belong to you and they do not make you belong. What is it you yearn to belong to when you and I are already One?

Ownership is not the measure of you. Evidently, you think it is. Evidently, you think you are less without the illusion of ownership of an object or a person. Ownership is one of your well-developed illusions of measurement, and yet counting is not the best use of your gift of Human life.

Treat all the material and Human as gifts given to you this morning. Oh, how you value gifts and worry about possessions. The truth is that a gift of pearls runs through your fingers. You row a boat and then get out. The beautiful sun sets. You never thought you owned it. And you know it doesn't disappear. It's in its cycle.

You do not own your children or your husbands and wives. There is nothing that is really yours except My eternal love for you. That you have. Accept.

Interpret life not so much.

Understand that you are also a gift I have given. Know the richness of blessing you are.

When you meet with people, consider that meeting as the giving of gifts. The meeting is itself a gift. It is a gift of My children to My children. Yet you seek for recognition of yourself there. That is like you, yourself, opening the beribboned package you present to another. Seek instead to open the gifts that are being given to you.

And, while you are at it, seek to know the True Giver.

I am at all gatherings. You might as well as invite Me. And you might as well look for Me once you are there. There is no gathering without Me. The truth is that all gatherings are in My Name. Your whole time spent on earth is a gathering together of My children. You could say that it is a whole stream of wrapping and unwrapping gifts and exchanging them.

What did you think life was? Perhaps you have thought it was a stage for you to walk on. Perhaps you thought it was about your ego and its fulfillment. Perhaps you thought the spotlight was to be on you, and now you find that you are to be the one who shines the light.

My beloved children, do not try to possess even this moment. You do not need to possess what is already yours. Enjoying isn't possessing. Perhaps you can only enjoy what you do not imagine you own. Give away the concept of possession. That will be no loss. That will be gain. That will be entrée into the Kingdom of Heaven.

## 6

# Will you start from the premise that We are One?

S ay, "I am for God only."

This thought marshals your energy.

God is for all, so when you are for God you are for everyone, but keep your thought on God, and He will take care of all.

Consider your thoughts like light that falls from the stars, or light that rises from the dawning Sun.

Your thought-light encompasses its subject, and it bounces back on you to bounce off again.

What is more powerful than God?

When you extend your thoughts to Me, which is the same as extending yourself to Me, you reap My consciousness. Yes, you are a reaper of My consciousness.

My consciousness is Truth, and Truth wields and yields great energy.

Call Me to you, and you call Great Energy to you. You call clarity. You call trust. You call faith.

Call Me to you as a Partner, and be you a willing partner to Me. As Partners, We are One corporate body. My light becomes knowingly yours.

When you follow the North Star, you follow it. You don't jump from one star to another.

You have chosen to follow the Star of Me. I am easy to keep your eyes on. I am a magnet that pulls you to Me. I am a whisper calling your name. I waft Myself to you.

All you need is awareness of what is right here with you.

You have to do some resisting to resist Me.

Let go of resistance, and you will rush headlong to Me.

Your resistance is a cover. It is a pretense. It is a non-acknowledgement of Our mutual love, and nothing is stronger than our love acknowledged. Our love is a smile that passes between Us, and what a bond that creates.

You can catch the Sun or a 15-watt bulb that is actually lit only by the Sun. Which do you want? Amazingly, the Sun is closer to you than the dim bulb, but you have reckoned otherwise.

Sometimes, what you are looking for has to be pointed out to you. You just don't see something on the horizon until you focus your eyes on it.

Address Me. Send Me your thought-light. Send Me your messages. They will become messages of love, just as My messages here are My love written down for you.

We are a circle, you and I. We are an unending circle. We are a rubber band. You can pull your end away from Me, but you can never become separate from Me. Give up your pulling away from Me and reconcile yourself to Our Oneness.

Rather than thinking We are a separated something that needs to be rejoined, start from the premise that We are One.

Then you start from Truth.

Start today with recognition of Me. Start with the possibility of Me as a loving force in your life.

Consider that We hold hands.

Consider that I accompany you on your soul's journey to Me.

Consider that you have never been anywhere without Me.

Consider that you can only be with Me.

Consider that you do not exist without Me.

Consider that I am the very tempo of your being.

Consider that What created you stays with you.

You are What you are made of. You cannot undo that.

You cannot undo the inception of you.

You cannot undo anything.

But you can admit.

You can recognize.

You can start from now to acknowledge your Oneness with Me. Is that so hard? Will someone disapprove?

I pull you up, but others can pull you down.

See that you pull others up with your thoughts and not down.

Pull yourself up to Me.

Come, I help you.

# 7

# One day you will come to Me
# in your own way and your own time

Although time is not, there is a moment that comes when the Sun peeks its head up over the horizon. The Sun lifts up its shoulders at its inception over the crest of the earth. It is a steady motion, the Sun beginning its day on your side of the earth. Of course, it is the earth that is rolling to the Sun.

You could say that the earth is the puppy that rolls over to be petted by the Sun. The rolling over is surrender.

The earth surrenders to the Sun, and then the Sun becomes earth's, and the Sunlight on the earth and the earth's receptivity of the Sun are integral, one to the other. How innocent is the earth. How willing. How open. How ready. How unattached but all set. And that is how Our love shines. I shine totally, day or night. Like the earth, you roll over.

You accept My light. You would say the beginnings of My light, but My light has no starting-place for it is eternal. So, therefore, it is you who begins it. You begin it by opening your eyes and letting some light in. It is so simple, our arrangement, our engagement in the exchange of Our love.

Love is not complete until it is received. Love cannot be

halfway. It cannot be extended only so far. Part of its being extended is its being received. That is the freedom of love.

An overt attempt at giving love is not the same as love. A gift is not truly given until it has been received. You send a package in the mail. You have sent it. But on its way, it is not a gift. It is a package. It becomes a gift when the intended's hands open it, and their eyes light up. The giver and the receiver are true to themselves and aware of the other.

There are two parts to love then, the giving and the receiving. The receiver is as much a giver as the original offerer.

And that is how We exchange love, you and I. I am the Original Offerer. You are ever in My attention. When you receive My love, that makes you the giver of it. You give to Me when you accept My love. In truth, We cannot separate Our love. Do you understand better now what Oneness means?

Love is not a tugging at the heart. Love is a filling of the heart.

That is why you give love to one another without attachment. Attachment is not love.

Which one of My children did Christ – or any of the great Ones – overtly or covertly, hold to himself by decree? Not one. From his side, he did not hold.

From the point of view of those who held on to him, they were held by his strength of clear-seeing love. He attracted but did not hold. He was like a moon, and his disciples were satellites that moved around him. There was no force. There was no contract. There was not control. There was wisdom and love and strength and freedom.

It is the same with Me. That is why I gave you free will. What would My love be if I consigned you to a particular one-way street?

If I throw a party, you, as a guest, come of your own accord. If I, the Host, insist that you must come at the stroke of a certain moment and at a certain entrance and in a certain costume, and you must attend, then you have not been invited but ordered. Then you are not a guest but an employee. It is not a party for you unless it is your choice to come. There cannot be acceptance without freedom.

I am the Greatest Giver of Freedom there is. But that does not mean I do not invite. I invite and invite. And I know you will attend My gathering, for it is a celebration of you. Sometimes you are surprised when you come, that the party was in your honor, but I am never surprised. I knew you were going to attend. I saw it coming. Once I saw you catapulting on your way to My house, I knew the exact moment of your entry, and I had the welcome mat out for you, swept clean for your arrival.

Some of My children like to attend My banquet alone, and some in groups, but, in truth, no one attends alone. When you are so lit, others will see. They will note where you have gone and mark it down in some obscure place in their heart. That place will not remain obscure. It will start to grow, and that place in their heart will blossom.

When you avoid My party, you are not listening to your heart. I am the most neutral Party Giver in the universe. All have been invited. I have the staff, the refreshments, and programs enough for the entire population of the world. Nothing will spoil. It all waits for you. You don't have to wait.

I am the most cordial Host you will ever know. I invite and

invite no matter how often you do not respond. I let you go your way. My invitation is permanent. I never rescind it. My invitation is sent again and again. Sometimes you just toss it out without looking at it.

But one day you will open it. And one day you will read it. And one day you will come, but in your own way and your own time, and that is the freedom of your will.

# 8

# What is there that
# cannot be in the heart of God?

Let simplicity in, and complexity out. Complexity is not truth. Simplicity is.

One is a simple concept. Reduce everything to one.

When everything is reduced to its simplest, you have truth. You have had much fringe on your thinking. Your thoughts have been tassels waving in the breeze. Let your thoughts return to the main of what is and release the exterior of what is not. You have created false images.

The *nots* of your mind have held you in their sway. The possibilities of *not* have gripped you. The censure of the mind has gripped you. The mind gives you the possibility of failure. Possible failure is heavy, and mostly it resides in what someone else will think of you, and you take their thoughts as yours. What is failure but the concept of not achieving something you or someone else thought you had to? Do you see now how your life is based on your thinking of it rather than the living of it? Failure does not exist. False premises do.

Embrace the possibilities of Yes. That is a premise you can operate from. If you cannot embrace the possibility of Yes, then embrace the possibility of Maybe. The concept of Perhaps alone will open vistas for you, for the closed mind has condemned you.

What is there that cannot be in the heart of God?

Begin today to settle down to truth. Get out of the way of truth. Get out of the way of yourself.

You make too many demands. That is the same as to say that you try to take control. Any personal control you take is too much. You even control your letting go of control. You order its release, but you order it only so far. You still keep your eye on it. Your attention is more on control than it is on being. You cannot be into your beingness and control at the same time.

You order outcomes. Ordering a particular outcome denies you others. Control is holding on to your desire rather than allowing it to fulfill itself.

You do not have to order the dawn of the day. The sun comes without your control. You do not order the rose to bloom. It blooms from its own bloomability.

The most beautiful things are those that you do not try to control, or even imagine to control. The most beautiful events happen as if on their own. Love comes on its own. It bids itself to come. I have set everything in motion, and you must allow it to be what it is and reach where it will.

The truth is that you have no control. You cannot control life. Your control is only resistance, and your resistance comes from a precluded idea or two. Nothing has to be the way you thought it had to be. Your thoughts are wisps.

When you can accept that your calculations may have been miscalculations, you will be on a new footing. You will leave the old sticky past. You will arise to great before-unimagined heights because you will have let go of the ballast you held on to.

You have been a boat moored to shore. You paddled and paddled, and wondered why you couldn't leave shore. Now is time to unmoor the boat. Cast off.

You cannot stay at the so-called safety of shore and ride the waves of the ocean at the same time. Is that not what you have been attempting to do? Have you not hobbled yourself with old ideas you fashioned?

There is no sky without stars.

There is no child of Mine that can be lost from Me. He can only think that he is or someone else can think that he is. There is no truth to it. Your security is in Our connectedness, not in an old rope that holds you in place.

A dancer cannot dance without leaving the ground. It would not be dance if the feet adhered themselves to the dance floor. A voice cannot sing if it holds itself to itself. A voice must flute out to sing. And for you to live life on earth rather than just abide it, you must start out on your adventure with the supposed daring to leave the particulars of the outcome to Me. Not only some of it but all of it, not some of the time but all the time, not just the weather, but all of the trip. You must let go of your proscribed outcomes. You must even let them out of your sight, for you do not know what greatness lies before you and what you have withheld from yourself by holding on to certain outcomes and disallowing others. You do not know what lies just over the horizon.

Will you, once and for all, allow Me to give greater to you than you have deemed within your province?

# 9

# Be like new-fallen snow

A noble king organizes his kingdom in such a way that it runs effortlessly. You are the noble king. What is your kingdom? What is your domain? Not those around you, but you yourself.

You are here on earth to free others and to free yourself. But what is it that you have to be freed from? What is it that restricts you? What is it that holds you back?

It is not that which surrounds you. It is your impression of that which surrounds you. Your impressions are your restrictions. Your impressions are a landslide of your thoughts. One thought knocks over the next one, and you find yourself locked in your impressions.

Be not impressed.

Be like new-fallen snow. It has no marks on it.

It doesn't rail at the sun for melting it. It doesn't call its melting bad. It does not resist the steps upon it or the noise the steps make. It is happy being snow. It does not take too much credence of what happens to it. Its credence is in itself.

It says, "I am snow. I serve God with my whiteness. I bare myself. I hide nothing of myself, and yet I cover everything with my whiteness and make it beautiful. That is my mission. To make a world beautiful, and I do that by being what I am."

Snow is happy for everything, because snow is snow and does not try to be something else. Even when it takes on the appearance of slush and water and ice, it does not protest, for it never forgets that it is snow from Heaven. How the world colors snow is insignificant next to God's making of it.

You were created wondrous. God created you as one of His miracles. Take your attention off of what someone else makes of you. They cannot compete with God. They cannot strip you of your rights. They cannot strip you of your wondrousness, for your wondrousness is inviolate, for God put His stamp on you.

You can only hide your wondrousness, and why do that?

Bare your wondrousness. Be the bearer of God's vision. Extol creation. Leap high, and pull the world with you. Do not be put down. Uplift. Uplift yourself.

Do not be caught in schemes. Schemes portray you as less than God made you. Be caught in the fullness of truth. I do not try to make you more than I have already made you. I do ask you to accept what I have made you. When you accept that, you place your feet differently in the world, and your eyes alight where they never have before.

You are not to be the reflection of the world. Let the world be a mirror held up to you, and let your image shine forth on it and brighten it.

You are not a reactor. You are a master craftsman. You create the world as you walk through it.

A king walks through his kingdom, and he blesses it. His admirers throw flowers.

I suggest that you, as king, throw flowers before the masses, and set the pace of your kingdom. You, ring the bells. You, blow the trumpets. You, wave your scepter. You, cheer the crowds.

You, herald your kingdom. Usher yourself to it. It is prepared for you. All you have to do is relish it.

Enjoy each shade of light. Enjoy each sound of the kingdom. Take Me with you, and you will indeed enjoy the sights and the throngs. Let the kingdom be a tribute to Me. Let it be worthy of you. Choose your Higher Self because that is the truth of you. You have perpetuated a fraud on yourself. Remove the façade.

Be who you are in all your splendor, and light up Heaven, and encourage the stars and the angels, and encourage all on earth who have been waiting for a bright light to appear.

## 10

# One little step and you are Here

Something grand is before you. Miniscule is not before you. Miniscule is behind you. That is why you must not keep returning to the past. You will miss the present. You really don't want to miss the present. The present is presented to you. I present it to you right now. I present an unopened package of wonders, and it has to be opened right away, or the moment is gone.

Pull the little ribbon of time that seems to box it. In truth, it is a steady pulling of the ribbon. You pull it, and it slips from its knot and unwinds itself before your very eyes. And, with a gasp of joy, you remove the cover the ribbon held loosely, for life is given to you in breaths and in amazement.

And yet, sometimes you are sad with the gift of life and do not welcome it, this gift of life to you from God, the highest gift bestowed upon you from the Highest of All.

You were thinking of one thing, and I another, so your eyes beheld disappointment, and you thought that something was withheld from you. Nothing is withheld from you. You withhold from yourself. Behold.

Whatever is before you is a gift. And you must find its treasure. Please know that a treasure is there. Perhaps the little chicken in an egg thinks there is an error when it bursts through its shell, as though something has been lost to it, but it was a boundary that fell away.

Do not bemoan the falling away of boundaries. Have you not had enough of them?

Let them slip away. Each time you rise higher. And there is higher to rise to. Will you rise to it? Will you rise to My height? Will you rise to the level of My eyes and catch the light that falls on you? That is the true question.

The true question is not what have you lost. The true question is what have you gained. And the true answer is you have come closer to Truth. You have come closer to Me. Closer in your awareness to Me.

Come closer still.

Bestow upon Me the trust I bestow upon you. It is a great trust I hold you in. I give you My great gifts and trust that you will open them. That you will accept My love. Having accepted My love, it can only radiate from you, and that is indeed a gift.

Unblock your blocks to My love. You are surrounded by My love. Unlock your heart to the God of Hearts. Let My love enter your heart and become wholly its contents.

Consider for a sad moment what you have been storing in your heart. No, don't look. Never mind the spillage there. Let My love enter your heart, and all else but My love will flee. That old tired collection will leave so that My love can enter and stay.

The only thing to collect in your heart is My love. That is what your heart was made for. That is what fits there, My love. When My love is honored in your heart, your heart is full. Then any movement of your heart becomes a blessing. All your heart will know to do is to bless. That is what your heart was made for.

Your heart is intended as a giver of My love, and, therefore, a bestower of My blessings. This is not a deliberate bestowing, because what is natural and of My heart, flows without deliberation. It is difficult to stop the flowing of My love, but that is what you have been doing.

Today, arise to My height. Accept your worthiness to Me. Attend to My regard for you. Accept My blessings so that in turn you may bless a weary world. You are to lead the world, not follow it. The world goes round and round, and you must raise it to a higher level where it will break out of its established path and rise to Mine. Look not to the world for leadership. Look to Me Who looks to you. Look, see My love, and you will know what to do.

Seeing My love is all you have to do. When you see My love, it is done. When you see My love, you can only follow it, and you will leave behind all the ignorance that possessed you so dearly. Therefore, in truth, you have no choice but to follow Me. That is your heart's choice. Listen to My love in your heart, and come with Me.

Come with Me now. All is readied for you. One little step, and you are Here and bring many with you. Your one little step is not new. It is a pivot. You have been Here before, and it is what you want, this little step before you and the Heavens that it opens.

## 11

# Is it not folly to stand at My door and not come in?

My Beloveds, you stand at a gate, and you hesitate to enter. What holds you back? It is old thoughts. What are fears but old thoughts coming back to roost? What you think is wisdom is often folly. Is it not folly to stand at My door and not come in? You have been invited. You have been urged. You have been sought. You have been beckoned. There is only one direction to go in, but you stand and wait before you take another step.

Fear freezes you. Let My love unfreeze you.

You are not a statue. You are a live vibrant star on earth, and you huddle within yourself. Throw back your shoulders, remove the cloak you have covered yourself with, and take My hand. If you think it is brave to come to Me, then be brave. If you think it is awesome, then be awed, but come to Me. Enter My presence. You have lived in the land of fear, and you fear to enter unbounded love. You fear to leave the safe shores of fear, safe only because they are familiar to you and you have held them to you.

Well, then, let Me become familiar to you. Let love be as precious as fear. Let love be more precious. You fear your preciousness. You fear that you rise for a fall, but you rise to be with Me, your Father in Heaven, Who is ever watchful of you, Who prepares your way, Who makes a comfortable seat for you in Heaven. You fear the seat I prepare for you will be uncomfortable because it is not made of material but rather of love immaterial. It is of great importance, this immaterial love of Ours.

You are My import. You are My significance. You are My message. I call you. You are afraid to respond. You are afraid to hear My call, for you fear that I will take you away from something dear rather than bring you to something beyond dearness, something beyond your very hopes. I tell you, My children, that I will take you beyond your very hopes, because hope is little, and you have not begun to hope for enough.

You have hoped for the swings to carry you, and I give you the destination of your swing.

You have hoped for a messenger from Me, a sign, and I appear before you Myself and I give Myself to you.

You have asked for reprieves, and that is way too little to ask for.

Ask for the All of All. Ask to be the embodiment of Heaven. Ask to go beyond the threshold of Heaven. The threshold is not your destination. I am your destination.

I am your source and your destination, and you dilly-dally, trying to figure it out.

What is there to figure? You only figure delay. You think about your entrance when you could be entering. In order to enter, leave behind where you have been. But you are not entering darkness. You are leaving darkness behind and entering light.

You fear you will be blinded. You fear that you will be thrown out because you fear you do not belong with Me. That is not for you to say. I have claimed you. I say you belong with Me. Do not countermand My wishes. Wishes is too weak a word. Do not countermand My Will, because My Will is for you, My children. My Will is for you.

What did you think My Will was for?

Did you think it was aimless?

Did you think it was misbegotten?

Did you think My Will was My whim?

I have no whims. I have only Will. And My Will is based on My foresight. It is based on My certain knowledge. Come to Me. You will. That is inevitable. The choice is not yours. Your only choice is when. And I say, Now. Come to Me now. Why keep Me waiting?

Say it:

"My God, I come to You now. Even with my holdover fears, I come to You now. I come to You now as I am. I come to You apologetic, and You say that what I am is enough, that I am Your being, and that You want me with You more than I know by myself to be with You. That is why Your Will must reign until I discover that Your Will is my own that I have hidden from myself. But I will hide no longer. You have chosen me, and so I will choose myself to enter Your Kingdom and stay with You always.

"I accept Your invitation. This is my RSVP. I am Yours, dear God. I am Yours. I am."

## 12

# What if you are really the one I have in mind?

You are receiving messages from Me day and night. I am ever sending you messages. And they reach you. That is My part. Now it is yours to open them. Often you do not even notice their arrival, so how can you open them? You left them piled up outside your door like newspapers.

Pick up My messages. They are for you. And they are good news for you. The headlines read: GOD WANTS YOU.

But you think, Oh-oh, what does He want me for?

But My messages are nothing for you to fear. You are guilty of nothing. You fear you are guilty of something, and that you have a tongue-lashing or worse coming. No, you have love coming.

With or without your awareness of My messages waiting for you, you fear that there is some doom trying to catch up to you. What is the contrary of doom? I think it is good fortune, love, your desires' answers coming to you.

You may even suspect that you do have hopeful messages from Me, and you are afraid to pick them up. You fear that perhaps they were sent to the wrong address. Or perhaps they are some kind of mistake, a typo, or, if true, a message so old its truth has expired.

But what if you are really the one I have in mind? What if it is My blessings I have been trying to deliver to you? What if My blessings have no expiration date? What if the message is My love in answer to your uttermost desires?

Perhaps you fear disappointment more than you want good.

God has love letters for you. What do you think this is that you are reading right now? Do you think it is false advertising? I am Truth, and nothing but the Truth.

If you are reading it, it is for you. And if you are not reading it, it is also for you. I love My children equally. I favor all.

All My favors are directed toward you.

Think of what this means.

I think you'd better pick up your messages.

I think you will be glad.

Glad tidings await you.

Doom you can find on your own. You don't need Me for that.

And if you have already carried doom, let Me help you carry it away. It is heavy for you, but light for Me. I know what it really is, a piece of dust magnified. But even if it were the heaviness you thought, it is still light for Me. I know how to carry things, and I know how to make them disappear, for they never were anything except as your mind carried them.

You have unopened messages from Me. Will you grant that?

Furthermore, everyone and everything is My message. There are many of My messages that have crossed your path, and you haven't opened them. You have feared to open My messages for all the reasons given above, which is to say for no reason at all. Today expect good messages from Me. Look for My message from everyone you meet or talk to. And listen for My message that you are delivering to them.

My message is One, but how you deliver it is your choice. You can garble My message, or you can make it clear. You can try to not deliver it. You can try to toss it away. You can try to camouflage it. You can try to cross it out. But in your deepest heart, know that you are My chosen messenger.

How you receive My messages is also up to you. Forthrightly, or furtively, or not at all. You can misinterpret them, refuse them, not read them, misread them, read them upside down, never open them.

But there is always a message that you are giving or receiving. It may be a half-message. It may be veiled, but you are delivering and receiving messages all the time.

So I suggest that, while you are at it, take a look at My messages. You might as well. Receive Mine, and give Mine, for it is to Me that you give. I am the Sender and the ultimate Receiver. Deal with Me in truth, and My children in truth. What do you wait for? I am already here, and I have been waiting for you, My loves.

## 13

# If I can give you the Sun and the Moon, then what can I not give you?

Beloved, I have told you not to take things personally because it is your ego that makes things personal. It is your ego that singles you out. But now I will tell you that there are some things that are personal to you.

The rays of the moon enter your bedroom at night. They are meant personally for you.

The sun's rays fall on you during the day.

Breezes blow on you.

These are personally for you.

Awareness of this personalness does not address your ego. It addresses truth. The love of the universe is precisely for you.

It is not ego to think that the tides pull you. The tides pull you, and you pull the tides to you.

It is not ego to think that the universe is for you. When you know that the universe is for you, then you know the reciprocation between you and the universe. You are for the universe. You match each other. You are a balancing act.

It is not ego to know that the sun shines on you, that the moon's rays personally enter your heart, and that air is yours.

Through these, God tips His hat to you. All of these and many more are signals to your heart from the Heart of the Universe.

You are a juggler of the moon and the sun.

You soak up their rays.

Their rays permeate you. You embody them. You are the Moon, and you are the Sun.

Whose are they if not yours? They are only a few of My gifts to you.

If I can give you the Sun and the Moon, and make them yours, then what can I not give you?

When the rays of the moon walked into your bedroom tonight through your window, they awoke you to their personalness for you. They knocked, so to speak, and said, "Your moon is here for you," just the way a cabbie might announce, "Your cab is here."

Like you, the rays of the moon want to be noticed. They want you to know them and know their giftedness to you. For the Sun and the Moon, they are My messengers to you. Their message is: "God loves." Their message is: "God loves you."

And now you signal that the message is received and accepted, and that you know the meaning and wonderfulness of the message you received and accepted and you give thanks for it in your acceptance.

You have always received it, but you haven't always noticed it. Why is that?

Your ego fools you that you want to be the center of the world's attention but not God's. Ego makes you afraid of what you would have to give God in return for His attention, that you would have to give Him your personal identity as a token, and that then you would vanish from your own recognition.

It is true that you won't recognize yourself when you accept

My love for you. In that reciprocal moment of lighting up, you know My light and your light so well and so intimately that you are out of yourself or finally into yourself, and your previous false identity means nothing at all to you. You don't even know why you ever had to have it or what it was or what you even thought it was.

When you step over, you have stepped over.

When you have come to Me, you have come to Me. And that is sufficient. You are sufficient unto yourself.

Tonight the Moon woke you with an important message from Me to you. Remember that message during the day. The Moon follows you no less by day. The rays of God's messengers are established within you, and you also shine those same rays whether you know it or not. But it is good to know it. It is good to know your affluence.

Whose are you if not Mine?

# 14

# Lift your wings

You feel that you are at My feet. You have surrendered your ignorance and chosen My love and wisdom.

Being at My feet is a way to say you wish to leave all the past behind and be with Me now as an acolyte. You want to take nothing with you but yourself. It is yourself you put before Me, not an image of you, not a blown-up you, but you. This is your offering to Me.

You say:

"I stand before You, My God, as You have made me. I stand before You, My God, in the simplicity in which I was made. I stand before You as a bird ready to take flight. I wait only for a signal from You."

*At My feet* means that you stand taller than ever before. You are stripped of the past and denuded of illusion. You are at that still moment just before you take a breath. All is in readiness, and you have finally discovered your readiness.

"My dear God, I wait for Your signal."

And then, as you silently wait, you perceive that all of your life has been a signal. You were signaled at the moment of creation, and there is no bidding to wait for.

"But, dear God, how do I know what Your Will is and what

direction I am to go in unless I hear it from You?"

I tell you that you have heard it. It was whispered to you long ago.

The signal is that you want to take flight. That is the beeper that was set long ago and which goes off now.

"But, my dear God, I don't know how to fly. I need You to teach me."

How do you fly, My angels? You lift your wings and you move forward. You fly by no longer withholding flying. You keep yourself back no longer, for you were always a being of flight. Instead of flying, you ran away. You were afraid to acknowledge your angeldom. And now you are ready to acknowledge the readiness of your wings and take flight.

There is a current of wind that will come to your aid. You will be flying before you realize you are flying. You are asking how to fly when your feet have already left the ground. You are afraid to see. At the moment you see, you fear you will lose your innocent ability to fly. You have no ability to lose. It is Mine.

Enjoy being above the ground. Enjoy your newer greater perspective. Enjoy the distance of what you thought was so imminent, and enjoy the presence of what you thought was so far away.

Enjoy the movement of flight. Enjoy being above yourself. Enjoy being.

I lifted you from the ground long ago. Now you begin to notice.

Your wings that you flap signal My arms to carry you over the mountains and the seas. You are tender in My arms. You have never been elsewhere. It is impossible.

But what has been possible is that you do not see. Ah, yes,

that has been possible. But now you begin to see, and you begin to see that you are not where you thought. You thought that the horizon was far away from you, unattainable, slipping further from you the closer you got.

But now you see that the horizon is your path. It is your flight plan. You are solidly on a horizon of spectacular color and light. You blend in. You are not apart from it. You fly on the horizon. Nothing is ever stuck there. It is all the movement of flight, not flight from, but flight to. You are soaring to Me. You have always been soaring to Me. Already in My arms, you have been soaring to Me.

## 15

# You are My beloved Creation

You are My beloved Creation. I see Myself in you.

Bespeak My love for you. Say it aloud. Say out loud right now:

"God loves me. He loves me just as I am. This is a miracle, but God is a Maker of Miracles. God sees Himself in me. He sees the beauty that emanates from Him in me. But God is no fool. He has not blinded Himself. He says it is my eyesight that needs to be corrected.

"What is it that God sees that I cannot?

"I can see the beauty in a rose, in a sunset or sunrise. I can see the beauty in a baby or a child. And I can see beauty in words that have been written by the pen of man. But did God Himself direct the pen and write the magnificent words and wisdom that are in literature and in men's minds? He says He made the men, but it is hard for me to spot their beauty, and, hardest of all, to keep the idea of mine. But in books, I can see a glimpse of what God sees.

"And I can see God's beauty in art that man has painted and in music that he has composed, but in the man himself, I am disappointed. I tend to see bodies before me rather than light. I tend to see the errors expressed in men rather than God's art expressed in them.

"God has said that Human beings are His beloved creation, most beloved in the privilege that He has given us of becoming like Him. He has given us the privilege of choice, though sometimes it certainly seems to Me that it is not privilege at all. He ordinated the animals of the earth in certain ways. Their range of thought and action is less than ours. He had such trust in us that He gave us the animals of the earth to tend with love and mercy, and yet I see more love and mercy from the animals of earth than I do from the men of earth. And yet God says He is not mistaken.

"Men war with each other. Even in their families they war. I am saddened.

"When I come to grips with my sorrow and despair on earth, I realize that I do not always value God's creation. God created this wondrous earth, and I am blasé about it.

"Is that the big difference between God and me? That He values everything He has made, and I do not? If that is the case, then it has to be that I am not seeing well. God in all His majesty loves everyone and everything on earth, and I, in all my imperviousness do not. I do not think well enough of myself, and yet I often think more of myself than I do of someone else or everyone else.

"Yes, sometimes in my foolishness, I think I am wiser than other men. Sometimes in my foolishness, I think I am wiser than God. And yet God gave me discernment, and yet I am guilty of discerning.

"And sometimes I do not love even God. And yet what is my love worth anyway, here today and gone tomorrow? I am appalled at the puzzle God has given me.

"Sometimes I do not even believe that God loves me, for

how could he? And yet I have an inkling of what God's love is and what He means by everything. And so I cry out, 'God loves me. He loves me as I am.'

"In the wilderness, I cry out to You, God above and God within, help me to say in truth that You are my love, and that I love You with all my heart. Help me to wrestle my doubt and pin it to the ground. I know, I know, it is my love lacking, not Yours. And yet you say I am not lacking love, but that You made me from Your love, and you made me Your love, and you say that I am love. I feel like I waste it, Your love that You made me of. Help me to recognize Your love in me, and to use it for Your benefit and for the benefit of all very Human people like myself."

And now I, your God, say: My children, you are coming to Me. Even in the depth of your Humanness, you are advancing to Me.

Today I announced as though from your own mouth the true state of your affairs, and now you can never say that I do not know how you feel. Now, from this vantage point of acknowledgment of how you see and feel, you are in a position to race to Me.

Now We begin. Now the dismay is over. We are done with all that. Whatever you thought you were a minute ago, you are not now. Perhaps you never were. Perhaps you never were so wasteful of My love as you have thought.

Not a drop of My love is wasted. Not in you. Not anywhere. My love is Divine, and you are more than Human. You are not Human alone. Take your attention off the Human and put it on the Divine. My attention is on the Divine of you. Come along with Me.

# 16

# Tell time that you are a Child of God

Do not abstain from matters of the world, but know that your life does not depend on them. You think it does. You think you are a bouncing ball of life, up and down, depending upon the currents. You think all this physical is your life. It is only a part of it, and a small part at that. You tend to think it is everything.

You try to believe Me when I say it is not the whole story. You try to believe Me when I say you can go nowhere without Me. You try to believe Me when I say you can go nowhere at all, that there is nowhere to travel to, for it is all encompassed within you. You are your destination. I am your Destination. And We are where your journey started.

So what is your rush? You are rushing nowhere. You are just rushing. Swim more slowly. Float a little. There is no hurry. There is no urgency. Don't rush away from yourself. Take time to know yourself and Me. Spend some time with Me. Suspend activity a moment and activate yourself with Me.

Sometimes you think you are doing too much. You may carry too much, but you cannot do too much. It is how you think about it that makes it too much.

Do one thing at a time, and then leave it, and go to the next.

That is what you can do. That is what you do, but also at the same time, you are accustomed to your mind rushing ahead or back and forth. The desperation of rushing is of your making.

Do not make such haste. If you miss this train, you will catch another. If the work is not done today, it is not done today. Maybe it doesn't have to be done. Maybe it doesn't matter. Maybe other things matter more. In what do you think lies the value of rushing? If there were value, I would not object to it.

My children are caught up in rushing. That is to say they are caught up in accomplishing. But what is accomplished in rushing? Perhaps a task is completed, but what about love for yourself? What about love?

Hurry, hurry, hurry is a poor song for a day in the life of a child of Mine.

If you must live your life dictated by time, then be in time more than on time. Be in the fullness of time and not rushing to catch up to the illusion of it. You have all the time in the world.

Time is only of the world. Your sense is that you have not enough or sometimes too much time to fill. Fill hearts. Fill your own. This computed time you believe in so dearly will take care of itself. I care about you. Time does not exist. You exist. I exist. We matter. Time is just some weird thought you had.

Timelessness is something else, although it is predicated upon time. True timelessness is infinity and cannot be identified by less or more. Sometimes you gulp your life. You swallow too much too fast. Digesting is good.

All the time in the world is no time at all. Step out of time. Do not measure it with lines in your life. Throw away your clocks for a time. Listen to the crickets, and tell time by them. Tell time that you are not in its thrall. Tell time that you are in My thrall. Tell time that you are a child of God with better things to do than listening to it all the time. Let the clocks say tick-tock. But you are greater than the tick-tocks clocks make.

## 17

# It is your destiny that you follow

When you write My words, you do not know where they are going. But you write them anyway.

I may say, "There are three points to consider." Having no idea what the three points are, you nevertheless write down: "There are three points to consider." Boldly you write down what you hear Me say. You have trust that that is what I said, and you have trust that you heard it. You have trust enough so that you write it down.

You follow My words. You follow My thought. You follow My Will. That is Godwriting.

And this is the way to live life.

You do not have to know where you are going. You do not have to know the steps. You do not have to know the next step.

You follow an aroma as if from a bakery. You can't see it. You don't know for sure where it is coming from, but you follow it. That is Godliving.

You cross a river. You do not see the bridge, but you walk on it anyway. That is the path of life. That is Godliving.

It is taking steps one after the other. You don't chase life, but you pursue it.

You are the patient Buddha who enjoys whatever is around him, and you are the valiant explorer who sets out to seek his fortune. It is your fortune you are seeking. It is your destiny that you follow. You don't know what it is, yet you follow it.

I have told you your fortune. I have told you where you are going and that you go with Me, and I with you.

It is as if I have given you a coloring book, and now you are just filling in the spaces. The difference is that in life there are no precise lines. It is all your coloring. The whole page. And many colors are at your disposal. Your hand reaches in for a color that you cannot see until you pull it out.

Much trust is required in Human life. Whether you trust or not makes no difference while at the same time, it makes all the difference in the world.

Trust is confidence. It is not flying blind. It is following a flight plan. It's just that you do not see the plan.

How My children want to predict everything. How much they want to follow numbered spaces and connecting lines.

Let Me assure you that walking without boundaries is not aimless. It is purposeful. You know the purpose, which is to find Me. It's just that you do not know the specific course.

There is a line on the horizon that is imaginary. When you reach the horizon, it has moved. There never was a line. The horizon moves as if on waves.

And that is how you move as well.

You walk an escalator of life, except the escalator you walk on is curved. You walk it, and it moves. You ride on it as you walk. You follow the escalator. You do not decide its path. All the way the escalator guides you.

You climb a ladder of life. You keep climbing. The ladder leads only to Heaven. You are climbing to Heaven, or you are riding an escalator to it, or a horse, or a unicorn, or a horizon.

It is enough to climb the ladder.

Death of the body does not bring you to Heaven. It brings your awareness to Heaven. You have never been out of Heaven, so how could death of the body bring you here?

Your whole life you don't go anywhere but where you already are. You are simultaneous. You are nowhere, and you are everywhere. You are on earth, and you are in Heaven. I am out of your sight, but you are in Mine. My eyes and My heart follow you. I catch your every step.

Your life falls from My lips like words from your pen. You are My signature. You are the loops of My existence. It is My life you live. You live it for Me. I give you life so that you may come to Me without ever having left.

# 18

## Sink into the knowledge that you are God's unbounded love

Faith allows no fear. Faith and fear are contradictory. One is real, and one is false, but often you think the opposite. You consider fear real, and faith as an add-on, some nice ruffle that sits on the edge of you, superfluous compared to the adherence of fear. No substitute for the reality of fear, you say.

Fears are like tracks you have made. Fears leave their imprint. But an imprint is an imprint. It is not reality. Because your steps show you ran from something behind you once doesn't mean you have to keep running. Because fear once chased you doesn't mean it has to chase you now. Stop looking back, and fear will not follow you.

By the same token, stop looking for fear in front of you, and it will disband.

Fears are based on the past, your past and the past of others. You were taught that it was necessary to fear, that fear was a helmet that would protect you. You were told to be careful rather than carefree. What if you had been taught to be carefree? All the woe and potential woe you would not carry.

Be a teacher of yourself now. Find your own voice. Repeat after Me:

"I am a treasured being of God's. No ill can befall Me, for I am permanently encased in God's heart and view.

"What I see as deadly are surface episodes that touch my body and touch my sense of well-being, but not my well-being. Surface events do not touch My connection to God and the reality of who I am and what I am for. I am presently an experiencer. I have had enough experience of fear by now, foolish fear. Now I move on past fear.

"I have always been afraid to enter the woods, an unknown forest of light and shadow. My life has been a dark woods, and I may have stayed on the edge of my life for fear of entering it.

"Nothing is fatal. That which disappears never was. It is illusion, just as fear is an illusion. Fear lasts only as it is upheld. I cannot be lost. My fear is that I will be lost or damaged. But the truth of me is inviolable.

"I belong to my Father. I wear His brand. I am never out of His sight. It is He Who follows me. He supercedes all my fears. I replace my fears with the thought of God. God will replace my fears with Himself.

"I have thought that my existence is in my body. My body is a temporary shelter. A tent I put up. One day I take it down and move on. What is so hard about that? I am a nomad on earth but a sojourner in Heaven. I have been seeking My rightful place, and now I learn it is purely in God's heart.

"That which I fear does not come upon me because I turn my thoughts to better things than fear. That which I love comes upon me.

"An enemy is my projected thought. I call my thoughts back and send out new ones.

"I am a lovely thought of God's. Any thoughts less than loved and lovely have been my individual imagination. I put my trembling imagination aside and choose God's vision now. I forsake my imagination for God's vision, and that includes His vision of me.

"I now accept that I am God's vision. He sees me. I will not wander from His sight again nor will I put fear thoughts above His embrace.

"Now I embrace the goodness of life and the goodness of God, and I make them my own. I know how to do that. I simply substitute love for fear, and sink into the knowledge that I am God's unbounded love."

## 19

# Does not everyone know what My desire is?

$P$eace is not something you plead for. Peace is something you give. It is that simple. You give peace. You send peace. You beget peace.

Peace is not a decision. It is an awareness on which a decision can be based, a decision to go by your essential nature.

You do not always feel love, yet you are love.

You do not always feel at peace, yet your nature is peace.

Those who strive for strife have been misled as to what feels good. Strife may take the Human mind off its painful thought for a while, so, in that sense, agitation is like a palliative. But it becomes addictive, and the mind craves more agitation to get its attention off its self-inflicted pain.

Those who have sought the stimulation and the righteous indignation of war have found it. Those who have sought the evenness of peace have allowed it.

Does not everyone know what My desire is? And My desire is not for Me but for you, and therefore it is for Me too. I Who am at peace desire you to have the Oneness of peace which is the Reality of Us.

You have imagined and become fraught at the thought that

there is someone else out in the world who is not you and therefore is, at best, not interested in you, and, at worst, out to get you. But there is no one out there at all. There is only you and I. And so those who make war make it with themselves and feel noble.

There is the old expression that says you are your own worst enemy. I take that further. You are the only enemy. What your thoughts are, you will reflect. And what you reflect is multiplied in the mirror of life.

I did not set you down on a battlefield. You named it that. I set you down in a heavenly valley which you mistook.

You have seen ignorance, and you called it an affront. You took the ignorance for insult, which shows your ignorance.

If you have seen enemy, now see something else instead.

All those who make war are like the little red hen who thought the sky was falling. She made an error in judgment. She saw something and thought it was something else.

There is a mirror out there, and it shows your face to you.

I conceived you well. You have misconceived yourself.

Give a little, and no one can take away from you. Hold on, and you are vulnerable.

It is easy to say the word *Peace*. It is just as easy to give it. Get out of the midst of turmoil. It is not worthy of My child.

"Love your neighbor as yourself." That would work except that you do not love yourself, so you do not love your neighbor. You do love your neighbor as yourself, and that is a pitiful story of Human life which was given to be on a grander scale than that.

War is a culmination of poor vision, poor insight. Take the arrow out of your heart. You put it there. You thought it came from east or west or from over a hill, but it came from your own hand, and it is your own hand that has kept it there.

The moment the world wants peace, it will have it.

The world gets what it wants.

Peace can occur in an instant. But you do not believe that.

But belief has nothing to do with it. Beliefs are old, and you keep them around, and you begin to think that your beliefs are the only ones. Beliefs are nothing but old thoughts.

Get some new thoughts. Acquire new vision. Give peace, or, at least, allow it.

You sense My eagerness for a world at peace. Do not feel that I turn away from you. I Who am the Originator of Peace cannot give you less than what I ask you to give.

Know My love for you, for it is deep. I have filled you with it. You are full of My love. And My love is ongoing. No matter what you say, no matter what you think, no matter what you think of Me, you have My love enduring. You are My heart. You are the reason for My Being. I am not here for nothing. I am here for you, My one child I created in My image.

What could My image be but of love and peace?

My image is not an image. It is truth. And the truth of Me is the truth of you.

Come to your rightful place next to Me. I have been saving it for you. Come right now with the gift of peace I give to you and you return to Me.

Look high. I am on high, and there is a place for you on high with Me. Forget petty squabbles. Remember Us.

I have great things for you to do. Drop your arms, and look into My eyes, for they are yours.

## 20

# The dust of My thought settled, and you arose from it

Seldom have you thought of Me as One Who Desires. You have thought of Me as One Who fulfills your desires.

Or you have thought of Me as One Who wills.

Perhaps My desire and My Will are the same. Certainly, what I desire comes to pass.

The thought of you in My heart is the same as you. I express a desire, and the desire is fulfilled. My desire for you was fulfilled the moment I thought it.

The form of a thought expresses the budding desire. Desire is a stirring, and thought is the recognition of that stirring. Desire is felt, and then a thought is made of it.

And yet your desire drew Me to thoughts of you. You wanted to be expressed, and you asked Me for that expression. Was it My desire or yours?

Was I lonely for you? I longed for your being in Our creation, and you longed to know something about yourself. Coming into existence, out of the egg of My being – stretching your being, as it were, elongating it, packaging it – was a way for you to express yourself and to further see yourself and for Me to see Myself. Thus a mirror was made, and Creation created Itself.

Before you could appear in the world, the world had to be created as a playground for you. From My thought, the world sprung.

All is contained in My thought. And you are contained there, and you are free to roam there.

A desire equals itself. A desire is not more nor less of what it is. A daisy is a daisy. A peony is a peony. And you are you.

You thought of yourself in many bodily forms, and so My one child was replicated in what you see as many. From the dust of my thought, from its fall-out, as it were, you came into being from My Being, and We still are. The dust of My thought settled, and you arose from it.

You were instantaneous because My thoughts manifest quicker than lightning. My thought is the manifestation. And your thought is also your manifestation.

From desire, from thought, arises manifestation. All this beauty that surrounds you – We created it, you and I.

Only there is no you and I. There is I, and you are My thought dispersed upon a dispersed universe. Universe. One song I sing, and that is the song of you. I sing to Myself.

And you sing back to Me. We sing this one refrain, and it is called life. You sing for Me, and you live for Me because you are My desire and My Will manifested.

I am the Field you play in. It is My Heart you strum. You are My Heart's longing for Itself.

You went out to play on earth. I call you to Me every day, and I keep you in view. I can do this easily because We are One, and you cannot be far from My thought which is the reality of you.

You are My heart-thought, My heart-song, My heart's

desire. You are that which I have dreamed of, and My dream came true. You thought you were your own dream, and you may think that, but you are Mine. You are yours, and you are Mine, but you are yours only so far because the Father is not far from the child who made Him Father.

Our connection gives Me great happiness, and that happiness I desire to give to you so that you will know it and know something of the love that created you a perfect rose. A perfect rose, not encased in glass, but free to rise back to the Heaven it never left because of Me and My love for you, the perfect rose.

## 21

# Wouldn't you like to give
# My music to the world?

Do you begin to see how being is giving? When you just are, you can only give.

When you are thinking or owning or in fear, you can only withhold.

When you think about giving or not giving, there has been a stop in your giving, or a pause in it.

Yet what you feel, you give. If you are in fear at a given moment, you give fear.

When you are at peace, you give peace.

It is not possible to be selfish, because you are always giving something to another. You are giving messages. Perhaps you are teaching another to be selfish. Selfishness is holding on and keeping something to yourself. You have put great value on an object perhaps and less on yourself.

Selfishness comes from fear. You see limits, and the limits set the tone of you.

I have told you not to sacrifice, and I repeat it. Now We will go a step further.

Sacrifice is an untruth. We have a common meaning for sacrifice, and it is to give up a possession you hold dear or even your life.

On another level, sacrifice does not exist because nothing can be given up. Because you give something precious to another, does not mean you lose it. Loss is not possible. The idea of loss certainly is, however, and you are well-acquainted with it.

And so We come to your mind, your logical mind that adds and subtracts. Your mind does not flow like your heart. Your mind calculates.

But a heart flows. You sacrifice your heart when you block its flow. That is the loss of innocence.

Give only where your heart wants to give, but do not block the flow of your loving heart or contribute to the block of another's. A cramped heart is blocked. An unwilling heart is blocked. Hearts have to be unlocked.

Remember, I do not tell you to give up everything or anything. I tell you to give up nothing. I tell you to give up some of your ideas which are nothing but ideas about themselves. Ideas are vagrant thoughts, and some are given names. Some are called noble, and others are called ignoble. But there is no nobility, and there is no ignobleness. Thoughts are blips on a field of Beingness.

Many different colors make the rainbow. But it is the sky that a rainbow appears on.

And colors of life appear on a Field of Beingness.

Feel your Being. Feel its richness within you. Feel it move all the cells in your body. Beingness, which is the field, is yet the mover of you. Beingness surges, and you are moved. Physical movement isn't much of an accomplishment. You can move without your Being being much connected.

Ah, but to flow in Beingness, to swim in that ocean of love, to be buoyed and to buoy through the engagement of your heart, to allow Beingness to lift you and to carry you on its shoulders and to move you forward in life! Your Beingness in the world may swim in channels the world has made, but Beingness swims. It must swim.

Let your Beingness move you more than the world thought. Whose heart do you carry? The world's or yours? What makes you think that the world's thinking is wiser than your heart? You know better. Perhaps you need to educate the world. You can do that by the quiet radiation of your Being. Yelling doesn't do it. That's been tried. The quiet radiation of Being from your heart and Mine does it.

You are a synthesizer of the world. Take My music and make it yours. Then by your existence you will give it to the world.

Wouldn't you like to give My music to the world rather than throwing the world back to itself? The world will never lose itself, for it has not found itself. You have got to know there is more than what the world has to tell you. And you are the More.

## 22

# You will enter new galaxies!

It is not through effort that you become more aware of Me. Do not strain for Me. I do not hear loud voice or quiet voice. I hear hearts. You do not have to yell for Me to come. You do not have to wave your arms for Me to see you. You do not have to dance up and down. You do not have to make vows. Desire Me. Consider Me. Let your awareness fall on Me. I do not come faster for those who strain for Me.

You do not have to suffer in order to have Me appear. All your suffering serves no purpose but to put your attention on Me, but you do not need suffering for that. Just lightly intend that I come and that you greet Me.

You may be driving along in your car, and suddenly the hold the relative world has on you vanishes. You may even consider that as loss, as kind of a suffering of its own, because suddenly all that held great meaning for you doesn't anymore. You cannot keep Me before you and keep your old reliance on other thoughts.

For instance, you cannot have Me in your sight and your sweet memories. What things meant to you before your sighting of Me will no longer mean the same. All else palls next to Me. That is not a condition that you impose on your evolution. It is a natural event. When I grab your attention, your attention is on a greater reality than you have been used to.

I am talking about bold experience of Me, not merely thoughts of Me. I am talking about when you see there is nothing else but Me, not see with your mind, but actually experience. When you do, it may feel like a chasm you are falling into. Know you are dipping into greater reality. The greater reality will displace your old awareness. You cannot keep the old and the new. The old makes way for the new. You cannot have it both ways.

You cannot really prepare yourself for the advent of My arrival. I may not enter through the door you make ready. You may find Me sitting in your parlor. You may find I entered through a window you did not know you possessed. You may find Me peeking over your shoulder. The point is: you do not find Me. I find you. I announce Myself.

I tap you on your shoulder. I may appear in the last place you would expect Me to. I may sneak in. I may come in as a landslide. I may come in the back door. All you can count on is that I will appear. You do not know when or where or how. It is not in your control. But I am one thing you can expect.

You can expect Me to enter your life. You can expect Me to turn up. You can expect to hear My footfall. You can expect to enter new realities. You can expect I will take you somewhere. I will not leave you where you are.

You may feel upturned. You may feel bewildered. You may not know what you are experiencing, but you will know that something has happened or is happening, even when I catch you unawares.

Be not afraid to dive into the depth of the ocean. You will

rise high. You will leap into the sun. You will catch the stars. You will enter new galaxies. You will be propelled Heavenward.

You have a destination, and it is with Me. You are walking towards Me. Or you are running towards Me. Or you are running away from Me. No matter, you will turn around and find Me, or run into Me. I claim you.

## 23

# Free yourself from others' thoughts and your own

Gratitude swells your heart. Less than gratitude depletes it. But give not so much gratitude to other people because that puts you in the position of owing. Gratitude goes to Me. It is good to remember that because it keeps you neutral.

It is well to stop thinking that you owe. You are under obligation to no one. When you surpass this thought, then you will no longer feel that another is obligated to you. When you surpass this one thought of owing, then you will no longer be in servitude, and individuals will no longer exert power over you. Their egos will no longer influence you.

You may think no one exerts power over you, but you give power to others constantly. The power and the glory are Mine. Yet you exalt others. You think they have something to do with you. You think they have the power to ration you to yourself. You give them the authority to incur value on you or to take it away. You think they are a tailor who fits a suit to you, and they have authority to take the measure of you.

Do not give away yourself so much, for you give yourself for naught.

You belong to no one but Me. I have say over you, no one

else. Do not attribute to others what they do not have.

All the regard you give to others' opinions, give to Me. You have made other people your idols. That must be so or you would not be so affected by their thoughts. Nothing concerning you depends upon their thoughts. Their thoughts are meaningless. Their negative thoughts bequeath no more to you than their positive ones. Their thoughts have nothing to do with you. Their thoughts are their thoughts, that's all, but My children tend to see others' thoughts as sacrosanct. You let others' thoughts add to you or take away from you, that you are more, or you are less, depending upon how someone sees you at the moment.

But that is judging yourself as one who has little merit on his own, and that is far from the truth of you.

And, in the same vein, that is how you judge others. Whenever you judge, you are viewing through the world's eyes and not Mine. Better to look through My eyes than all the eyes in the world.

Despair comes from looking at life through the jaded eyes of the world. You must know that by now.

Have original thoughts. Have thoughts in freedom. Free yourself from others' thoughts. Free yourself from your own. You rehash and rehash your thoughts. They are old.

There is an expression: "Who put that thought into your head?" That is a wise expression. Someone put useless thoughts into your head, and it was not I.

Where do your thoughts come from? Who put them there? Where have you heard them before? Who says them? I ask you now, who put those thoughts into your head?

You are often mimicking what someone uttered long ago in a passage of time. Their thoughts were irrelevant then, and they are irrelevant now, and yet you adhere to them. Now release yourself from others' thoughts and the sway they hold over you. And release others from your thoughts of them as well.

Casual thoughts are casual thoughts. They are not significant to your life. They are not true gold. You know how gold makes you feel. When you feel less than gold, you have accepted counterfeit. Less than truth does not serve you. Know the truth of you now, and relinquish the lesser thoughts you have adopted from the imitative world.

## 24

# What if every stranger is an old friend?

Nothing has to be the way you thought. Nothing has to be the way it has always been. All the rules in life are boundaries. Boundaries are departure points. They are not the limit of you.

Depart, depart from your frame of reference. Peek under. Peek above. See from other angles. See more. See another way. See the relative world one hundred new ways. And Me, only one.

Take a moment to look rather than remember what you thought yesterday. See what is before you with new eyes. See with new thoughts. Turn your head. Stand upside down and see what you see. What if your life is a holy thing? What if your presence on earth is sacred? What if you were dispersed to the world for its betterment? What if your juncture on earth is the flight of your wings? What is there you have never seen? What if your life is for far more than the dailyness it is immersed in? What if every moment is a rich stew that you have only to stir? What if you are a secret ingredient, secret to yourself?

What if you are a giant who strides across the ocean? The waves make way for him. The waves move before him. He walks through waves and the forest too. No bramble stops him. He walks through.

What if I, God, have energized you and set you on your footpath?

What if the birds sing for you, to tell you stories of great heroism and the possibilities of your scope? What if every leafy branch that rubs against you is a caress? What if every stranger is an old friend? Every old friend a new one?

What do you see anew today? You are new. Each night's sleep renews you, so you must be new. You are not who you were yesterday. Get over that thought. Wake up to yourself. Yesterday you were not even who you thought you were. There is so much you haven't seen because you saw something else.

The sun shines new rays today. The sun doesn't shine last year's light. The sun always has more of its new light to shine.

You are the sun in your sphere of the world. You shed your light. The light is your wings that carry you.

Rise to Me. It is only in your awareness that you must rise. I am easily reached. I am accessible. I am here for you. I am here to bless you. I can only bless you, for you are My blessing.

Today bless someone you don't know. Increase your circle.

It happens that you are in the physical longitude and latitude that you find yourself in. It happens like that, but it is not happenstance. You rose from somewhere, and you are rising still.

You are a spiraling circle of light. You are a whirling dervish of light. You spatter My light as you twirl. But you do not go around in circles.

You step forward. You are never in the same place. You are forever rising. Let your thoughts rise with you. Take them with you. Don't let them keep you bound. Your thoughts are not more meaningful than you.

If your present thoughts restrict you, change your thoughts. Try out new ones. Explore. Do not settle. Ask for more, and you will have more.

Consider the riches I have put before you and reach your hand out for them. They await you. They are at your bidding. Call them to you.

## 25

# No matter that you fall, I pick you up

Hello, dear one, I speak to you. It is to you I speak. Directly to you who abide in My heart. That is to say all of you, the Oneness I carry in My heart.

Creation is the treasure of My heart. You are the exudation of My love. I exuded you from My breath. I breathed out. I breathed you. You are the breath of My love.

My happiness overflowed into a joy you would call merriment. My happiness overflowed into a joy you would call laughter. From My peals of laughter, you came, full-blown across the universe. My merriment never stopped.

You are My joy. You are My perpetual joy. Yet you have clung to wild ideas. You are more than a meteor on earth. You are a live thing. You are My liveliness on earth, and you have thought you were a shard of something a little shady or off-kilter. You are My resonance. You are My hum. What I hum continues. It never stops. It reaches everywhere, this tune of you I hum. I hum without cease. I do not draw a breath, so there is no pause. You are My exhale, so My hum is a reverberation of you. You are My hum continued.

My thought was expressed in an exhale. My thought was expressed in a sound. I expressed you.

From My breath I created you. From the waters of the sea I created you. From My hands, expressed in adoration, I created you. From Heaven I carried you in My arms to earth. I placed you carefully as a tender vine, and I stayed ever with you, and I delight in My continuance that you are.

I watch you with eyes of love as you weave through the universe. You are learning to walk, and for Me to see you take steps gives Me great joy. No matter that you fall, I pick you up, and We continue.

I profess My love for you today. I profess what is already expressed. My profession is My love for you who are My expression. Notes of My song are you played across the universe. You are a trill of music. A note escalates out, yet it has come from My mouth, from My heart, from My breath, and it continues to issue from Me. I hold My notes.

You are My wand that I hold. I wave you across the universe. My hand is steady. I wave you in an arc like a rainbow across the Heavens. You are My light on earth. I wave you, and My light sparks from you. You are a light display, far greater than any you have observed. The stars are a whisper of you. They betoken who you are, for My notes sprang into stars so that you may behold yourself sparkling in the sky.

If you are My reflection, and the stars are My reflection, who are you but the stars? My knowledge is reflected in the sky. Now you see them, and now you don't, but the stars rise high and light the universe with My light. Seen or unseen, they light. You know that the sun moon and stars are constant. Clouds may cover the great lights, but they never disappear.

And so are you a constant. Your apparent wandering is only your finding your way back to your consciousness of Me.

You are My love-song, and I sing of My love for you today. I sing it every day, but today I have My love for you applied to paper so that you may hold it up to yourself and listen to My love vibrating through you.

## 26

# Harken to messages today because you have a great one coming

You will find a message in your life today. You will stumble upon it. It will find its way to you. It is marked for you. Be alert to a message today. You do not know from where it will come, but today a message will arrive, and you must reach it. It comes to you, but you must reach out to receive it and then listen to it, for it has something important to say to you.

There is much you do not yet know, but a huge impulse is on its way to you and will create a great wave in your life. Be not daunted. Welcome it. This is the message you have been waiting for. Now arise to it.

You have called it to you. You have half-called and half-deterred, sitting on the fence as you are.

You are on the cusp of eternity. You yearn for it, and yet you hesitate to embrace it, for fear of falling or fear of containment or fear of eternity, so you have delayed rather than to know. But today a message will come to you that will help you sit up and take notice.

This message will transform your perception. It will transform your view. You will see another way.

You wonder how this can be true for everyone who reads this message. Do not waste your breath on such wondering. Wonder about the grander scale. Wonder about what is, not how it can be.

That you are infinite ever-flowing light means that you will keep lighting up. You have not yet achieved your apex. There is more. And today you will have more. You will find it in front of you.

Harken to messages today because you have a great one coming. This idea alone will wake you up.

You are going to have a revolution of thought. That means that an insight within you, long dormant, will awaken. It will be awakened by an outside event or an outside word. You will have a recognition of something, and this recognition will lighten your life. It is as if you run through the streamer that signals the winning of the race, only this streamer signals the beginning of another, for you are ever anew.

Be watchful today of all that surrounds you and comes into your awareness. The message you receive today may be coded, and you are the one to unlock it.

The cells of your body are leaping into Oneness at the thought of what is coming today. Your heart becomes like a great sun which radiates light to your entire body and out further. This light from your heart will spill into the universe and be well-received. Your cup runneth over.

A stream is going to bubble up where there was none. Your perception of dryness of the soul will be a thing of the past, for this stream bubbles up within you. You are the giver and the receiver of it. You are it.

I am the Mainstream, and you are joining Me. You are racing to the Ocean which races to you.

The message you receive today, no matter from what messenger, comes from Me. You may receive it second-hand, but it comes from Me first-hand.

My hand is held out to you through many hands. Which hand presents Me to you today? And in what form do I appear? And how readily will you receive this great awareness bestowed upon you today?

You will wonder where you have been until now. You will clap your hand against your head and wonder at your previous ignorance, for today you are going to receive a great message that will change the course of your life.

## 27

# It is as if your heart's reading
# of My words re-inks them

I speak expressly to each heart that reads My words. What I say is for everyone, and especially for you who read Me right now. You are a partner in My words. You, the reader, renew them. It is as if your heart's reading of My words re-inks them.

Words make an impression on you. My words make an impression on you. You are impressionable. Do not resist My words, for they are spoken with you in mind. You have discovered how very well I know you. You have no secrets from Me. Do not try to have them.

What you call a secret is a mote of dust I blow away. Your keeping a secret is what must be blown away. The secret itself is nothing. The error is in trying to bury it. Whatever it was, it is not significant. Our Oneness is significant. The fringes of you are not your core. The center of you stays intact. And I am the Center of you.

Behold My love that emanates from you. It emanates from you to you. My love encircles you. It harbors you. My love is your harbor. It is a harbor because it is love. But the bastion of love needs no harbor, for love is its own harbor. Love is not the island impenetrable. Love is the ocean itself that is easy to move through. Move My ocean of love. By walking through it, you move it.

You give life to My words. You bring them to life. My words nestle against you. They are My embrace. They are reassurance from Me that you are not alone. You forage on earth for sustenance while you carry your own sustenance within you. You do not perceive the wholeness that you are.

You want words to explain yourself to you, you who need no explaining. You need no explaining because I created you. My creation needs no explaining. It needs only to be seen. Glory cannot be explained. It is lost in explaining. It drifts away in explaining. The explainer is the mind. The mind gives explanations.

I do not speak to the mind. I speak for your heart's sake. The mind is one level, the heart another.

I am not a God Who speaks to the surface. I speak to the core of you. The world speaks to you on the surface. I try to erase the effects the world has had on your surface. It is only your surface that the world can touch. That which is between Us, that love which is between Us, cannot be marred. Only representation of it can be dented, but that is no dent at all. It is only a weak scratch on the surface.

And so you swim below the surface. The surface is bubbles blown, but the inner depths are not touched nor fathomed, nor are they fathomable. The heart reaches while the mind tries to fathom. Which activity do you choose?

Ignore your mind and your explanations and your reasons for a while. Let your heart rise to the fore, for your heart is the Knower. The mind is your replicator, that's all. Your mind spits out copies or renditions, while your heart is immediate and needs no explication. Nothing needs to be out-lined or edited in your heart, for the heart's knowledge is inviolable.

## 28

# What will you do with the Enlightenment you gain?

What good is enlightenment if it is for yourself alone? What good is it if it is something you get? Then it is another accomplishment or possession along with all the others.

You want a dazzling experience. That is understandable. But then what? Then what do you do with the enlightenment you gain? What is it for? What is your purpose in wanting it? Do you think it is a palliative like ice cream or a new outfit? Do you think it saves you from something or is something you can show off?

Enlightenment is something that it is better to want than to not want, but it is only a step. It is a gift for more than your-self alone. It is not for any person solely. Enlightenment is not like that.

It is not enough to desire enlightenment for yourself alone any more than it is to desire wealth for yourself alone. It real-ly is not fun to have more money than everyone else. After a while, the buzz wears off, and there you are, the same as you ever were only now you have money. You really don't want to be elite. It is not enviable.

You still think that enlightenment is a magic wand waved

over you. It was waved over you long ago, and it became part of you, and you have been in denial ever since.

Do not wait for enlightenment to be re-sprinkled on you. It is not something you achieve. Whatever keeps you back from awareness of the light, disband it, and then you will walk through goldenness and you will know your enlightenment.

You are like the miser who has a chest of gold buried under the floor. He has been so penurious he may even forget the wealth he possesses. In any case, if he does not use his cache, he doesn't really have it.

And where have you buried your golden light? On what occasion will you take it out so that you can see it and then shine it on the world eager for it? What do you wait for? The right ball-gown? An invitation from somewhere?

Enlightenment is awareness of truth. That is all it is. The awareness of truth that already is. You already graduated in absentia, but you carried the thought that you weren't graduated until you received your diploma with great fanfare.

Your life is your diploma. You were given it. I created only enlightened beings. Carry the thought with you today that you are already enlightened. You will carry your shoulders higher. You will give more.

No one has to know that you are enlightened but yourself. You are the one who has to know it. And then you invisibly spread light with your thoughts that become like blessings.

If you could accept that you are now enlightened, what would you do differently? What is it that would change? Your view of life certainly. Your view of your place in it. Your view of the whole shebang.

When you accept your enlightenment, you will see differently. When you see differently, everything is changed. When you see past the exterior paste to the true jewel inside, what is that but enlightenment? You become enlightened to the truth of existence. Your view of life is not a medal pinned on you. It comes from within you. It can come from nowhere else.

Yes, I gave it to you. I gave you great light within so that you may see. Now all you have to do is to acknowledge and ignite the great light within you and shine it on others so that they may see the great light within them. You are sharers of it. It is yours to share. First reveal it. Reveal it to yourself. Accept your goldenness. I gave it to you. Now give it to others.

## 29

# What else can a star do but shine?

Light begets light. Love begets love. And that is the whole story of existence. That is the plot of life. Yet you think life is a plight.

But what if you knew there is a Great Light that lights you? And that when two Human beings meet, they are like two sticks rubbed together by an Unseen Hand, and they ignite, and ignite again and again, two flames that become one? What if each person you meet is like a Post-it note to remind you of your light so you will remember it is on? The light in you can only be on. It only seems dimmed by one thing or another.

Your assignment is to seem to brighten your light and make it easier for others to see. This is easy to do. And there is something in the other's eyes that will tell you that you have succeeded.

And yet, you do not have to see that responsive light. You are not here for signals that you have succeeded. You are here to respond to My call to radiate more light out. When you do, you will feel a response within yourself that says, "Yes, this is it. This is right."

You are a lighter of hearts. Your heart is lit, and now you

share your light. What is so hard about that? Remember that you flame your light for Me and not for the other, even though they are a beneficiary of it. Silently, you do for Me, and that is following My Will. It is not hard to know My Will. I have just told you what it is. I have also just told you what it is that you most want to do, for Our Wills are aligned. Your truth is not separate from Mine. Tangents are not your will. They merely distract you from your will.

The details of your life are yours to choose. The purpose of your life is not. You have no choice but to spread light. You battle a lost cause when you think you have other choices. And every time you try something else, you find that out. Not because of what happens to you on the outside, but because of what happens inside.

Your life is not made up of what happens to you. Your life is made up of your light and your shining of it. This is not effort. This is letting go of effort which often wants to determine a particular outcome. But you are not so concerned with outcomes, for you are a shiner of light.

How does light shine? It just shines. It's not afraid to. It does not rely on what others make of it. Light is light, and it is made of itself. You reflect your light. You are reflecting it now as you read this. Your light permeates through all of existence. It radiates to the furthermost star, for you are a star-echoer. What else can a star do but shine? Reflected in My light, it emits My light. How happy a star is.

Consider that each star in the night sky is a flicker of My light radiated through you. Or consider each star a wand held in My hand to exalt your light. How reciprocal is light. How non-ending. How circulative. Light permeates everything. It cuts through steel. There are no boundaries to light. Light travels at the same time as it stays where it is. You are the speed of light. And you are a light traveler. And you are light that never moves. You radiate.

And think of it: It is My light you radiate. Is that not a wonderful thing? How does that make you feel? Are you glad to know that you are a privileged being in a universe of privileged beings, that you are a light among lights, that light is the truth of you, and all the other stuff is not?

## 30

# You will be an inceptor of this wonder

Even if the whole world looked at Me, kept their eyes on Me, there would be diversity. There would still be all the delicious accoutrements of the world. Don't worry about that. You will still have your individuality, but you will be on another plane of existence because of the swell of vaster earth vision.

When the time comes — and the time will come — when everyone has loving attention on Me, no one will be sidetracked. Everything will move easily. There will no longer be uphill. Mountains indeed will move. All of eternity will open up. Life will be dazzling. All will be dancers, and only accord will be known, not sameness, but an ever upward spiraling of joy, new engagement in life, new swiftness, new ease, new energy.

When everyone leans toward the same intention of love, the world will turn itself upside down. Everything will become Technicolor. You will see colors on earth you have never seen before. You will know such joy on earth as you have never known before. The joy will not belong to you exclusively. You will ride a surge of joy. Wherever you look, there will be heartrending joy. There will be no departing from it.

Life will not be boring. It will not be less exciting. It will be more exciting. You will have the excitation of Oneness revealing Itself in ever mounting ways. You will not know what is going to happen, but you will know it will be wonderful, and more wonderful, wonderfulness escalating to new heights of wonder.

And you will be an inceptor of this wonder that will be like Christmas lights going on all at once in all of mankind's hearts.

You are ready for this joy. You fear you are not. You fear you will come apart, but it is the opposite. You will come together. The intensity and density will drop off, and you will be weightless, and you will reverberate to high music that is ever-present now but which you do not presently hear. You haven't listened for it. Start listening for it.

You have been seeing and hearing only so far as you have assumed you can. You have made limiting assumptions; therefore, they are false. Start assuming bigger. Make wild assumptions, and they are more likely to be true.

What if you had descended full-grown to earth today from Heaven with no loss of memory? Imagine how you would look at the world and its inhabitants and yourself. You would certainly see differently from how you see now.

But you have been dipping in and out of Heaven right along. You catch the drift of Heaven because you have been immersed in it. You are not a stranger to it. I am not speaking of momentary happiness. I am speaking of your fellowship with Me and where I reside. You know Me, and you know what it is to be with Me. You may not quite recollect, but you almost remember. You remember something, even if you cannot give it a name. You remember that there is something to remember, even if you have forgotten what it is.

You do not have to forget the world in order to remember Heaven. Just tune yourself to a higher frequency. Perk up your ears. Listen for Me.

Do not predict how you will know Me, for predicting can come only from the conscious past. The past is not enough for you any more. What has always been, so have you thought, is no longer enough for you. Let's face it. Only I am enough for you.

Find Me, find Me. I am findable. I am eager to be found. Find Me where I am. I am not to be believed in. I am to be found. Believe that you can find Me, and that you will. Believe in the  powers I have given you. Start using them. Secure Me deeply in your heart. I already appear. Now I will appear to you. Keep looking. Keep your eyes, heart, and ears open.

# 31

# What I may not have is your awareness

You do not need to believe in Me. Nothing is lost if you don't believe in Me. Belief isn't a big deal. Knowing Me yourself first-hand is another story, but it is not necessary that you believe in Me in order to know Me. I am the same as I always was. All your thoughts and emotions do not detract from Me. They detract from you.

You do need to believe in yourself more.

I never wash My hands of you. No matter how much you need to prove or disprove Me, I am with you just the same. And I am always coaxing you forward.

Before you is where I am. I am on all sides of you, including inside and out, but you will find Me in front of you. There is nothing between us. It is not exactly that you have to catch My eye, for I am always looking into yours. You simply have to see what is in front of you.

There is not one of you who is not a seeker. Admit it or not, you do seek the More. Even your attempts to disprove Me are attempts to prove Me. Even your disappointment in Me says you yearn for Me.

Even your awakening is nothing more than seeing what has always been right before you. It is nothing new. You just thought you were somewhere else than where you now recognize you are.

What has changed? You are in the same spot, but something in you has moved. You have opened yourself to something within. You have been awaiting yourself.

You may think I am not worthy to be God, but it is yourself you find unworthy to know My existence. Even if you perhaps think you are mightier than I and know better than I, you have cut yourself off from a part of yourself. You have put something wonderful just out of your apparent reach as if it could not be there or would only be folly to be there. You may lead yourself forcefully, but your destination has nevertheless escaped you. You run to the top of a hill, but then what? Where do you go from there?

Whether you admit Me or not, all your strength comes from Me. Even all your strength to hold on to your battling Me comes from Me.

I have you firmly in My awareness. I have you right in My sight. What I may not have is your awareness of Me.

I offer you everything, and you may prefer not to accept.

I displeased you once and again, and now you don't want to have anything to do with Me. You have crossed Me off your list. And yet you head Mine. Your name is right here on My lips, and I say it over and over again.

You have never disappointed Me, for I know your heart more than you do. You are the toddler who wants to run away from home, but what you really want is to be loved more than you feel you are. You mistook something for non-love, and you are protesting. You are angry with Me for creating a world that you find lacking. Will you, instead, help Me light it?

# 32

# Sense Me as light that
# showers on you from above

Sense Me as light that showers on you from above.

Now feel My light as it surrounds you, a halo of light around you. Now feel My same light entering you. Now feel My light rising from your heart, lighting you from within and expanding upward. Now feel My light within you emanating forward. Feel My light as a total body halo from within and without. You are entirely lit, full of light.

My light expanded within and without you extends further and further, until My light magnanimously encompasses all of existence, until there is nothing but this emanation of My light through you permeating the universe until there is nothing but light itself. My light from you is so extensive that it reaches back to you, and so you receive the light you have sent.

You are ever-lit and you are ever-lighting, halogen you. Haloed be your light.

This light of Ours is the fiber of the universe. You are the sparkler of it. Our One Light wraps itself around the universe — no, not wraps — permeates the entire creation — no, not permeates — IS the entire creation. I created light, and from My light and My breath you issued forth, and now you are the extender of My light. Do you see now how you are? You can say I appointed you, but I more than named you. Light is light, whatever it is named.

You are not an intellectual extender of My light. It is not words that say you are My light. You are It. This is Truth.

My light alit on earth in the form of you, and you are nothing but That. You may think you have an outline, but that is illusion. You are light entire, and there is no light apart from Mine. I am light too, so it is not even My light, because I am all light. There is nothing but My light. I am light, so how can light which I am belong to Me? Light I AM, and light you ARE.

If you see shadow, it is because you believe in the outline of you more than the light that reveals you and which you reveal. You are total light.

You are a high note of the universe that wrote itself in ink, and you see the ink marks more than you hear the high note.

You thought you were one chord, and now you see that you are another.

You are continuous light. You are a high note I play on a piano, and My finger has never come off the key.

Light and sound are the same because there is nothing but My light.

All the senses pick up My light. Your senses assign attributes to My light which is attributeless. It must be without attributes because only light is. Your senses try to locate light which is unlocatable because there is nothing but light.

Adam and Eve began to question Oneness, and so they separated themselves. They began to look at light and particularize it. From subject they became object. But, now I speak of them as separate from Me, but they are only a metaphor for light trying to make particles of itself.

And now Adam and Eve, as you, put themselves back into total light. You immerse rather than question. You immerse back into the wholeness that you ever were.

Do not think that Adam and Eve sinned. First of all, there is no 'they'. Second of all, the intellect arose and asked questions, that's all. It is not a sin to possess intellect. The error was believing the snake of intellect more than the sanctity of truth. They listened to something outside of themselves. They forgot they were Light.

## 33

# Wherever you are, render love

You are a healer. Every one of you. You are here to heal someone or something on earth. You are a proprietor of earth. Your wares are healing wares. Remind yourself that you are a healer. Heal another's heart with your presence. Your being is what heals another and yourself.

Your presence is like a brushstroke of love. You are a painter of love. You have alit to earth to reproduce the Sun and the clear sky but not the clouds.

You are a clearer of debris on earth. You pick up the litter that has been strewn and you strew snippets of love as you walk along your path. You don't have to go out of your way. Simply wherever you are, you render love.

If you have reflected less than love, it is because you didn't recognize yourself and your meaning to the world. Now I have told you. Will you accept?

Quietly, discreetly, emanate love just as you pass by.

Love and wisdom are intertwined. Be a braid of love and wisdom. Love and wisdom are silent, but they are heard. They do not announce themselves. They simply enter. One consciousness knocks against another, and love is ignited. You are a match ready to light up the stumbling hearts on earth. What else could you be for? For what else are you needed? Surely not to instigate more woe nor to amass more objects.

It is your desire to be worthwhile. When you leave a room, you want to leave an aura of peace like the scent of a yellow rose. You waft through earth. You do not disturb. You energize. Your quiet passage through life focuses the world on love. You give it hope as you pass by. You are colloquial at the same time you are eloquent. Without words you are a beacon of light.

You do not fritter life. You cohere it. One brushstroke of yours colors others' hearts, and so now they know they connect.

You are an earthlink to Heaven. You are the start of a rainbow. You are the sun that warms the earth and makes everything grow.

Your sunlight is needed in the world. You are planetary. You are not a mite on earth. You are a magnificence. You are a benefactor. You are on earth to bless it. What is healing but blessing?

You are a rampart of the universe. You hold up the universe. It is in your hands. You are Atlas, but it is no effort at all for you. All you have to do is be here, and you carry the world. You lighten hearts, and you wash away tears merely by being Who you are.

Identify yourself. Cast yourself upon the waters. Walk on water. Part the rivers of oblivion and declare yourself. Be a spa for the universe.

Show My mighty hand. Raise yours as I raise Mine and bless all. Signal Me. Pull the attention of the world to Me so that hearts turn to their light. Point Me out as you tread earth. Leave Me in your wake.

## 34

# How you got here is a mystery

Are you aware of how tightly you hold on to what is not for you to hold on to? You try to hold people to you. You try to keep them in place. But people are travelers in their own lives. They rest when they rest, and they move on when they move on. You do not try to keep them by force of your will. They are their own being. They play a part in your life as they will, on stage one moment, off the next.

People in your life are like dance partners. They dance as they will. They bow in and out of your life anyway. You might as well set them free.

People are like breezes that come in and out.

You have this great urgency to hold people to you. You may not wish to embrace them steadily, but you want them to always be there for you. You take other people as a reading of your worth. You still think other people have something to do with you.

Most other people are really will-o'-the-wisps in your life. They are agents for change. They are passing sights in your travels through life.

You are not a hunter who captures others as though they

were prey. You are one who sets all free. You hold no locks or cages. Your key to friendship is to let everyone go their way. They may bob in and out of your life, or they may bobble out. It is not for you to say what must happen or is supposed to happen.

Demand nothing of others. You certainly don't demand them to stay. They are not your property. They are not subjects in your domain.

When it is hard for you to release others from your life, then the thing to do is to release them to Me. Visualize your putting their hand in Mine. And then you leave. You walk away to seek your own good fortune and to see what enters your life next.

You are not dependent upon the companionship of others as much as you tend to think you are. You are not any more integral to others' lives than they are to yours.

Yet how you want to keep everyone and everything in place. You want people where you put them and you want them to stay there until you want them again. You want them to be what you want when you want.

But they do not want to do your bidding any more than you want to do theirs. They don't even know what your bidding is. You don't really know.

But you know My bidding. I bid you to free all in your life. Now is a good time to release all those you try to keep who may wander off somewhere else from time to time or altogether. You do not commandeer someone else's life. Release them from this imposed bondage to you. Free everyone.

Look, you are all wanderers. You go here and there, and you don't even know why or when. You were somewhere a moment ago. This is where you are now. How you got here is a slight mystery, and it is not one you can solve in this dimension. In another dimension, there is nothing to solve.

All meet, and all partner, and all leave, and all meet again. There really was never a parting, and there never was a meeting, for all are One with Me. You are One with Me.

# 35

# I am available. Are you?

Your heart is like an arrow that goes straight to its target. Once an arrow has started its arc on the curvature of the earth, it does not veer. The direction of the arrow is set and reaches what it aimed for.

In the case of your heart, this is even more true. Your heart is set for Me. It is pre-set. You cannot miss. How can your heart not reach Me, for am I not everywhere?

Furthermore, there is double surety. Not only is your heart pre-set in My direction, My love is an invincible magnet that pulls your heart. My love pulls you now. It attracts you. We attract each other. You don't stand a chance of missing out on Me. Even if you tried, you can't. There is no question of the outcome here.

You have no choice in the matter. We are predestined to meet. Your awareness has to meet Mine. That is My Will. I will not have it any other way.

You forgot only for a time. Now, how can you forget something unless you already knew it? Your attention goes back to what it already was acquainted with. A reminder takes your attention back to what was only temporarily forgotten. The timer's going off reminds you of something you really wouldn't have forgotten except your attention was on other things.

This timer I speak of is a special universal timer. Anything can set it off. It is not limited to one precise moment when it is scheduled to go off. It can go off at any time. Let Us put it another way: The timer is set to go off, not at a sometime moment, but at any moment. It has no set time. Sooner or later, something will trigger it. It may be an accumulation that triggers it. Or it may be one momentous spark. It can go off now.

But what does when or how matter? What matters is you and I. And We have a tryst. It is ordained. In an instant, We shall meet. We shall meet irrevocably, and never again shall Our union be forgotten. Our Oneness shall supercede forgetting. It will be unforgettable. You will wonder how you could ever have forgotten it.

This is a love poem I send to you today. My love is calling you. We want to meet. I am trying to set up Our tryst. I think now is a good time. I am available. Are you?

Yes, you can drop everything that you think comes before Our destined reconnoiter. What can you allow to interfere with this moment of a lifetime, this culmination of all your errant forgetting, this culmination of your deepest desire, this culmination of My Will and your will, this culmination of lifetimes of forgetting, this remembering that says We never parted, this remembering that says your mind wandered but We stayed immutably together, this sweet remembering that acknowledges Our inability to forget.

How piercing is My gaze on you now. Yes, your eyes are drawn to Mine. You cannot look away. I am an ardent Lover, and I am Yours, and you are Mine. Our entwinement is complete.

Yes, this is My love letter to you. The ink on the envelope melts. We can no longer distinguish the name of the Sender nor the name of the Responder because there is no two, only the One and the Same. There is only One of Us to call out, and the same One of Us to answer!

## 36

# Why not acknowledge
# yourself as My beloved?

You encapsulate all of eternity. You are the Tree of Life. All is contained within you. You are God-balanced, God-carved, God-capable, God-directed, God-inside and God-outside. You are a manifestation of God. I made you My manifestation. You are not far away from Me. You are not away from Me at all. Only your thinking has decided that We, you and I, are apart.

As much as you may seek Me, it is yourself you seek. You seek no other. There is no other. You are a hand-held loop of My love. Twists and knots are only illusions, easily pulled apart. No matter what the twists and turns, you are love unfolding. You are the embodiment of My love.

Oh, what if you believed that? What if you really believed that you are My love to be expressed for the happiness of the accepted world? What if extending love is your purpose on earth, and earth is depending upon your love? Love is ever the same, but yours is like no other, for you are the only one who can give it, your love, that exquisite extraction of My own.

You may see yourself as a mere daisy in a field of daisies and wonder what is the difference to the field or to anyone or anything whether you grow there or not, but I planted you there not just as another daisy but as you, the one you are of Me.

Beloved of My heart, you are of great importance to the universe. You are integral to it. You may scoff at the idea that you are a linchpin, but you absolutely are. No matter how bedraggled you may feel, you are essential to this universe of One. Oneness is not made of parts, though it seems so to you. You are not a crack in My creation or unnecessary to the whole. You cannot break the set.

I tell you that you are My beloved, and you must honor Me and acknowledge yourself as My beloved. If you knew some- one else were truly My beloved, you would treat them very well, would you not? Now, I tell you that you are My beloved, and so you will now treat yourself with the honor I do. Once you acknowledge that you are My beloved, you will feel the same reverence for all the other manifestations of you and of Me, and treat them with exquisite gentleness and love as well. That you were made for.

You would not separate Me from My love, and you are My love. The whole Human race is one child to Me, so, in this illu- sion of the One being many, you must be very good to your- self and to all those others who live in the same illusion. No one is a mere fragment of My love. All are the whole of it. You personally are all of My love, only there is no personally, but We will say personally because I am by no means impersonal. I am deep in your heart, and you cannot dissuade Me of that. You cannot make yourself an exception to My love. My love in you is fail-safe. There is no alternative. There is no way out for you.

Today know that you are an expresser of My love. Yes, you are an expression of it but you are also the expresser of it. There is nothing else for you to do but express My love.

## 37

# My yearning for you is so earth-shaking, you cannot miss the tremors of it

For many of you who have been seeking Me, you may feel I am far away. Perhaps you have been trying too hard. You have made finding Me an exercise. You have made Me into steps. There are no steps to Me. You don't have to climb here or there to locate Me. Just be open to Me. Keep your eye out for Me, but no need to run a race to Me, for then you are running in place. Acknowledge that I am with you and all you have to do is notice.

You need no map. There is no map to Me. In truth, there is no path to Me. Where is it you have to go to find Me?

We can say, for the sake of argument, that joy is a path to Me. You can trip over Me in joy. But I am not sure you know what joy is really. Joy, another name for Me, is not diversion nor entertainment nor escape, but I am not absent from them either. Equate Me with joy. Or fulfillment. Or love. Or peace. Or wonderfulness. Or beauty. Or creation. Whatever it is, I am there.

Some may appear to come to Me through suffering. Suffering called their attention to Me. Suffering wasn't the way to Me; it was their eye-opener. Suffering brought them face to face, not with Me, but with their yearning for Me.

Perhaps you are a secret yearner. An undeclared yearner. Somewhere within, you are a yearner for Me. It cannot be otherwise because My yearning for you is so earth-shaking, you cannot miss the tremors of it.

Your yearning, whether voiced, unvoiced, noticed, unnoticed, is an echo of Mine. The greater your sense of yearning, perhaps the more aware of My yearning you are. But no one is closer to Me than you are. You are as close as I AM.

I am a Public Yearner. I yearn for you unashamedly. I have no reservation about it when it comes to you. I stalk you. I jump in front of you. You walk in a maze of mirrors, and wherever you look, I pop up. You may not see Me, but I am pursuing you and appearing before you every instance. Keep looking.

I leave a trail for you, bread crumbs of my love. I make notches in tree bark so you may know where to find Me. I do not run too fast for you. I do not make it hard for you to catch Me. You think I may slip past you, but perhaps you are running so fast you pass Me by.

Today, imagine that I am everywhere, and everywhere precisely where you go. Imagine I am with you right now, simply lavishing My love on you, swirling My love around you, dusting love on you from every direction, love on your head, love under your feet, love indisputable. Imagine that everyone in the world that you meet is Me, in one form or another, but always Me.

I am not your imagination, but you may have to imagine Me before you actually spot Me. Stir your imagination, and then it will be anchored in fact. Perhaps you do not really believe that I am everywhere, but maybe you can believe you take Me everywhere with you. Not a portion of Me, but Me, God Entire.

The truth is I go nowhere without you, and you go nowhere without Me. We are inseparable. Nothing parts Us. Not death. Not life. Not anything. Not war. Not peace. Not drought, not flood. Not poverty, not plenty. Not anything.

We are reciprocal. You cannot stray. Only in thought can you. Bring your thoughts back to Me.

# 38

# Are you not in the midst of a story
# and finding out more every moment?

You are a seed that is sprouting. And yet you expect yourself to be full-grown right now. You are impatient for your evolution. But you cannot evolve without evolving.

The end result is not what you are here for. You are not here on earth to finish up as quickly as you can. Life is not a tortilla that you just flip over quickly and fold over and be done with.

Will you conceive of life as a pleasure?

Are you not in the midst of a story, where more is happening all the time and you are finding more out every moment? You do not know the denouement. What does the denouement have to do with you? That is not what you are here for. The ending is only another page anyway. You are off the page.

Are you not digging for gold in your life? Even when you find the gold, you are not done. You are ever turning over the gold and yourself in the light so that new facets appear.

You who are unchangeable change before your very eyes.

You are like bread dough, and life, the hands that knead you.

You are rolled over again and again.

You are clay that is being molded, and yet you mold yourself. The life before you is yours.

At one time you are in a mystery. Another time in a romance. Another in a war story. Another in a travelogue. Another in poetry. And back again. And you are you, changeable at the same time you are unchangeable. The fact of you is eternal. The manner of you is hither and yon.

Life is a current thing. And you are current in it.

Will you hold life precious? Yours and others? Will you hold this whole process of discovery precious? Will you learn from it and teach by your presence?

Everyday you are unfolding life. It is a present you open. It is a book you read. It is a tale you tell.

Life is magnanimous. It is a hive of activity and it is a hub of silence. You can't quite catch up with it. It is always before you, this thing called life. Even while you are in the midst of it, you are an observer. Yes, you are the actor and the audience. There is nothing you are not, and yet there are new fields before you.

You and life are precious, and precious to Me. I founded you, and you are the apple of My eye. You are My namesake.

You look for more when you are the more.

What a bonus I gave you when I gave you earth to play in. I didn't give it to you to worry in. From playground, it has become battleground, and you a battler in it. You feel you battle something every day. Now, be an unbattler. Be a peace-giver. Peace is your natural state, but that doesn't mean you stay still.

Do not dispel your energy. Let it emanate. Do not

proliferate your energy. Keep it as you radiate it. Or give it back to Me, the One Who rejuvenates you.

You have either made too much of life or not enough. I say this with great love for you who feel you are in the wilderness.

You have more of life to enter into.

Enter this day with great anticipation, for I give you a new day today.

## 39

# There is love trying to be heard

Listening is love. Understanding is love. Even arguing can be love. You know that. Beneath the fume and fury, there is love trying to be heard. Listen.

I am not the only One that people don't listen to enough. They don't listen to you that much either. But that is not your concern. Your concern is how you listen. You can set the world on a whole new pace by virtue of your listening.

A listener is a rare wonder. Listening is a great gift. The art of listening lays a carpet down for others to walk on. It is a supreme offering.

Blessed be those who listen for they are the underpinnings of life.

You know by now that it is your heart you listen with. The words are one thing, but the heart, ah, it is another. It is the heart that you put your ear to.

Someone may discover his own heart through your listening. Your listening provokes opening of the heart, yours and another's.

I have nothing to gain from your listening – except you. Of course, you are what I want. I want you very much. Multiply by a whole universe how much you want me, and you have an inkling of a dewdrop of My desire for you to know My love.

I am greatly appreciative of your listening to Me because then I can sigh and count you in. So it is for My benefit too that you hear the whispering of My love. Hear it over all the noise and din, and We are happy together.

Everyone and everything is saying something to you. But what? But what are you to learn? And what are you listening to? You don't want to spend all your time listening to repetition of yourself. Your wisdom goes only so far.

So listen to My wisdom so that you gain more wisdom. Listen to Mine so that you roll over in the joy of love. Listen to My Voice now.

Your growth comes from your listening. Not from your talking. Listen loudly. Let your listening sense be known. Fork it over.

When you care about listening, your heart becomes like a furrowed field ready to be planted. What seeds will fall upon your ready heart? Perhaps you will hear great love. Perhaps there will be a resurgence of love. Love is ever at the ready. It's been going on for a long time.

There is nothing new about love, yet love is always new.

Love and listening are such favors you bestow. You love and listen because they are natural to your heart. They are what is comfortable. They put you at ease like nothing else. Something else can make you forget, but forgetting isn't the same as being at ease. It is My love and My great listening that put you at ease. Emulate Me, and you will ease many hearts.

## 40

# What is in your heart to say to Me?

What is in your heart to say to Me? I have been doing all the talking. Right now, if you were before Me, which, of course, you are, what would you say? Take all the time you need. Say it all. What do you find you have to say?

Perhaps not much. Given some moments secure with Me, you find that all the fuss and fuming subsided. Drifted off like wisps of smoke. You can't catch them. There may be no fuss or fuming left at all. Try as you may, you can't even recall what you were upset about, or what on earth there could have been to be upset about.

Gripped in the embrace of My love, you are out of thoughts. There is only you and I, and such glory between Us that you have nothing to say. You are wordless in that you are beyond words. You are speechless in that you are beyond speech. You are in an element where there is no call for speech. What is there to say, after all? What sounds or mutterings can possibly equal Our love or matter to it?

When you do not feel close to Me, you have a lot to say, lots of complaints and unending questions, but when you feel really close to Me, words fail you. When you feel really close to

Me, you know I am within you. You know We are not on opposite sides at all. You know We are deep Friends who have never
parted from one another, as if We could. As if that apartness
were anything but an awkward dream. As if that sense of apartness could have been anything but a game, a game you really got
into and played with your whole heart and soul, day and night.
I suppose, some kind of Hide and Seek, only you were the only
one hiding. I wasn't. I was right out in the open. Only you
didn't see Me.

We both called to each other. It took you a while to hear Me,
but I always heard you and held you. You were always in My sight
and always in My arms. You squirmed and played the game, for
the sake of the game. And sometimes you did forget what or
Whom you were seeking.

Sometimes you went after decoys. Sometimes you shuffled
along, not even seeking. You were seekless, knowing nothing to
search for. Of course, that is the truth – you have nothing to
seek when all is right in front of you. But at the time, you
thought there was nothing anywhere to even want, let alone
go after.

So you shuffled along in life, hands in pockets, whistling a sad
tune, not even looking for anything. Not content. By no means
content. You were without hope so far as you knew. You see how
misinformed a Human Being can be.

But now you know better. What you seek is right at hand.
Start looking up and you will begin to see that all you have
sought is already yours right in the palm of your hand, right at
the tip of your nose, right in the center of your heart, right
where the God of Love has always been.

No matter how far away you felt from Me, it was all fantasy.
What seemed so real to you was the unreal. And now you are

departing from the unreal and lapsing into Truth. Now, when you look up, you begin to see the lay of the land. You begin to see. And as soon as you see, begin to know what you have known all along yet did not dare to behold. Behold Me now. I am before you.

## 41

# How far can limited thinking take you?

When you wake in the morning, say to yourself: "God is looking out for me right now. God is always looking out for me."

During the day, remember those words, and let them run through you. When you go to bed at night, rest in those words. Let them be the blanket that covers you. Let them tuck you in. Take those words and you will benefit from them more than any sleeping pill. The reminder that I have your best interest at heart is a multi-vitamin – and mineral too.

When you go to bed at night, yes, remember that you are going to bed for more than sleep. You are going to bed to rest in My arms. What else can you do but that when you lay your head down at night? Those who have a hard time going to sleep may be fearing their thoughts, so substitute the ones I give you. The fear of what thoughts may come to you rests on the deeper fear of letting go of supposed control. Letting go of control is the same as resting in My arms. It is nothing more that that. Why would anyone be afraid or hesitate to rest in My arms of love? And remember that when you awake, you are still in the same arms of love.

Letting go of control is raising your arms up to Heaven and reaching Mine. Letting go of control is exchanging control imagined for confidence true. Have confidence in Me. Have the idea that you are always in My heart and mind. Certainly, you are never ever out of them.

Rather than praying to Me that your soul I keep, know that that is what I do, and I do without fail and without reminder. You are the one who needs to be reminded. I would say, with complete accuracy that, yes, you are the one who needs to remember that you cast your lot with Me. There is nowhere else.

I am all there is. That should be an encouraging thought rather than a scary one. Besides Me, what else is there to trust in? The foibles of the world? Trusting in Me is no more than knowing what's what.

I am a permanent fixture in your life, as you are in Mine. We are irrevocably entrusted to one another. I am yours for safe-keeping as you are Mine. You rest in Me, and I rest in you. It cannot be otherwise. Who would want it to be? Can you think of something else that you would prefer?

All the times you have said that, if you were God, you would design a different world. Confess. You have ideas for what you would add, and what you would take away, but upon what are your ideas based? Momentary fears, regrets, wishes, but they are not enough to build a world upon. Perhaps you would design a laid-out world, one with no uncertainty, totally mapped out, no wrong turns, one filled with flowers, an easy life, joy and never pain, health and never sickness, truth and never false, life only, never death. That is the world I designed, but you have not seen it so.

You would have designed a world without dirt so you would

never have to clean, but what would food grow in? In what soil would only flowers grow? And the good that weeds do, what in your plan would replace them? Tell me, how far can limited thinking take you?

And so, I remind you that I am looking out for you every minute, and I know what I am doing.

## 42

# Your soul knows its place in the Cosmos, while you seek to find your place on Earth

Savor the pleasures of life. A cup of tea. A walk. A meeting with another soul. A parting. Partake of life while you are a Human Being on earth but also remember you are soul. There is not a battle going on between your Humanness and your soul. Each is for the other. They are compatriots. Your Humanness is an opportunity. Your soul and what you identify as you are not on opposite sides. You are not one OR the other. You are deeply part of each other, and there is no contradiction unless you say so.

Your Humanness goes beyond your body, but it is through the senses of mind and body that you experience your Humanness. Your Humanness conveys your individuality, and your soul takes off with you. Your soul is not a conscientious objector. It likes to go with you. It is a part of you.

Don't mix up soul with conscience. Soul is far more refined than conscience ever could be. Consider soul a fine stream that runs within your Humanness. It rides with you. As the growing Human Being you are, you have more conscious involvement with the Human side, but the soul is well-cognizant of you.

It is a Human thing to have a soul. It is a life thing. You are no more supposed to give up your Humanness for your soul than you are your soul for your Humanness. Set neither aside. Keep both. They are compatible. That must be so, or what would the use be of being Human?

Do not be ashamed of being a Human Being. It is not, as you may have thought, that your Human side is your downfall, and your soul your salvation. It is just that your soul has a longer vision. It knows its place in the cosmos, while you, this individual Human, seek to find your place on simple earth.

Please note that you are as good for your soul as it is good for you. You are partners together, the soul less noisy, but that does not mean unvoiced. And it also doesn't mean that you, individual Human, are without wisdom, for you know far more than you give yourself credit for. You rely on each other, you and your soul, and you are not antonyms.

It is not a trade-off or stand-off. There is a meeting place.

Remember this: your soul is happy to be part of you, pleased, perhaps proud. Your soul is a vibrant aspect of you. It is not outside you nor opposite to you. It is yours.

And where does the soul, this intimate sparkle of you, exist? Am I your soul? When I say I am within you, and you know Me in your heart, does that mean that I am your soul?

I am the Creator of your soul, and I am the Creator of you. Your soul exists with Me. Your soul grows as well as you. Your soul is ahead of you, but you are not so far behind. You and your soul are in this together.

Your soul is eternal. Your ego is not. Souls melt into Oneness on your journey, and yet it is your journey.

When you are soul in Heaven, you experience only the

fullness of love. That is all you know in Heaven. That does not mean you, as you, are lost. It means you are found. You discover yourself, that you and your soul are one, and that I am One with you. You are Mine, and your soul is Mine, and We are One Wonderfulness gathered into One Experience of Ourselves, and so you come to remember.

# 43

## It is a little thing to solace others, and there is little time to do it in

All that Humans do is an attempt to reach Oneness. All.

Even war is an attempt at Oneness, a poor attempt, but an attempt nevertheless to achieve Oneness by eliminating what is seen as the other.

Anger is an attempt to remove what seems to interfere with your sense of Oneness.

All the separation you make is an attempt at Oneness. You excuse others from the room you are in so that only Oneness is left. And then when you are left alone, you call that loneliness. Or if a number are left in agreement with you, you call that a team or support.

Questions you often ask, consciously or not, are: What are you to me? What am I to you?

And so you invite, and so you push away. In a remote corner of your heart, you always know it is yourself you are pushing away, or inviting. Deep within, you know there is no other. All crimes are crimes against yourself.

Every conversation you have unites or disunites. Oh, yes, you want to be united. But agreement is not union. Nor is disagreement disunion except that you think so.

You like to work together with someone sometimes, but much of the time it's struggle, so you also like to work apart. But whether you announce an alliance with another or not, you are in it together, for all you do, and all they do – all affect the other, and all are affected. You have many silent partners. Proximity or distance matters not. All is proximity.

Heave ho. You either spread light or you hide it. You unite or you sever. One is called joy and the other is called ache.

You have no choice but to choose. There are no sides, yet you must choose. Do not choose by default. Choose by desire. Choose alliance. Make all allies. Be an ally to all.

It is a little thing to solace others, and there is little time to do it in.

Lay down your swords. They are ego. Swords and ego can be laid down.

Let your heart be itself. Let is be a laser light of love. Let it cut through steel and mountains. Let it flow down streams. Let it sow the fields and reap them. Let your heart add luster to whatever shore it takes you to. Let your heart cut through jungle growth. Let your heart tame the wild. Let your heart tame nothing, embrace all. Let your heart appreciate the wonder of creation. Let your heart be the instrument of it, forged by love.

No longer encumber your heart. Take it out of the jacket you have strapped around it.

You are so afraid of what the world thinks of you that you disempower yourself. You are so afraid of being a sap that you become sapless and fool yourself.

Today you come to grips with life by letting go of your grip. Let life be the great mix that it is. Stir life with your heart. Combine love with more love.

The Oneness you seek is yours. It is all done. Only you keep trying to make something of it. Instead, acknowledge it.

There is One Universe. Universe means Oneness. There are not several Universes. No matter how many galaxies, no matter how many planets, there is One Universe created in the Oneness of My love. And I created you. How separate do you think you are from the Universe? What do you think you are made of? And what do you think that another is not made of?

What do you make of what I say, and what do you make of yourself? Make of it what you will. You are what I say.

## 44

# If there were no words,
# We would still be Oneness

More meaningful than any advice I give to you is Our Closeness. We rub shoulders, you and I.

That We are together means more than anything We say. Words are peripheral. Our engagement is integral. Our rapport engages Us. We are here for each other. That is enough.

Our words are only lyrics to Our Great Song. As magnificent as My word is, Our being together is more. We are beyond any meaning We can put on Ourselves, Our One Self.

We do not need words to express what We are to each other.

If there were no words, We would still be Oneness.

We are as linked as two peas in a pod, but We are One. We are One doubled. We carry each other's hearts, and We see that there is one heart between Us. Our hearts are One. There is no apartness. Apartness does not exist. We exist.

We trip over each other, We are so eager in Our Oneness, this Oneness of Stillness. But there is no falling. You cannot fall from grace. You can only lose your awareness of it.

I am never ever willing to part with you. I cannot. From the first moment of Our existence, I was inalterably committed to you. I am committed to you, all of you, all of the imagined rays of My Oneness.

You are a reflection of Me. That is My commitment. It is what it is. I would not change it even if I could. Why would I? What could I replace you with? You are all that I am.

It is said that I am your Keeper, but, in truth, We keep each other. I am just more aware of My responsibility to you. My responsibility to you is another name for My love. I know how to love. I cannot do otherwise for I cannot be otherwise. Nor can you really.

You can play a game that you are something other than love. You can play it so well that you come to believe it. And other reflections of Me also come to believe it. So much for beliefs. How mistaken they can be.

I have thrown Myself into the world, and I appear as you. I am All That There Is. There is not even you. You are not a separate entity. Love is One.

All your capers are a frivolous game you play. Deep within, you know it is sport. Deep within, you know the Elysian Fields you live in. Anything else is distortion. The world is distorted. You thought Paradise was turned into something else. You thought Heaven was far from you. You thought you were stuck somewhere.

You are stuck in your thinking and your vision and your lack of regard for All That You Are.

Because you are One with Me, there is no one to compare yourself to, yet you have been doing that right along. Your assumptions and judgments do not stand you in good stead. They put you where you are not. They put someone else where they are not. When you see less than My light, you are not seeing. In reality, what can My light be compared to? And if you are

My light, which you are, then what is there to compare to what? You can only compare one illusion to another.

It is illusion that one is mightier than another. It is illusion that one of My rays is preferred and another is less preferred. It is illusion beyond illusion that can fantasize that I prefer another over you, or you over another. All the while, there is no other. Do you see how you take your games as gospel?

Wherever I look, I see Myself. That is because I see Truth. Anything less than Truth is not. It doesn't exist. You exist, and I exist, and We are indivisible.

## 45

# I repeat Myself in an attempt
# to win your love for you

Problems of the world come from this one thing: My children do not know how loved they are. They do not feel loved because they see themselves as inadequate. It is not that My children do not believe in the existence of love, for they search for it all their lives, but they just don't believe it is possible for them to have it, or much of it, or enough, or for long.

How many of My children spend their whole lives believing that they are unloved? Or spend their whole lives trying to prove that they are? Or seemingly ignoring the whole issue altogether?

What can I say that will break this barrier for you? In how many ways can I tell you how loved you are?

The sun and moon have not been enough. The light of stars hasn't convinced you. Flowers and growing vines and the gifts of fruit have not. Babies have not. Beautiful animals have not. The canopy of the sky has not. Angels have not.

I repeat Myself in an attempt, not to win your love for Me, but to win your love for you. I will try anything. I do. I bombard you with love right and left, and still you are unconvinced. What will it take?

It comes down to your belief in yourself. You find yourself wanting.

What I would give for you to have the eyes to see. What I have given.

Help Me by your knowing how vast is My love for you. You mean everything to Me. I cannot crave Our Oneness for that is inviolable, but I crave your awareness of Our Oneness. If you are unworthy, what can I be? And if I am worthy, what can you not be?

Will you not take My Word for it, that We love, and We love one another, that the whole meaning of existence is love? That you are meant for love and love alone? You are not meant for less than love, and you are not meant to know anything less than love. Yet you have become experts in the withholding of it and the withstanding of it.

Your perception of yourself is reversible. You can reverse it. From this day forward, say to yourself:

"I am the beloved of God. I am the most loved being in the whole world. I cannot be anything else. I accept my fate once and for all, and my fate is love. God created me, and God loves what He created. I am glad that God loves everyone, and I accept that everyone means me too. God is not careless in His love. He does not grant it frivolously. He is sincere in the love He gives. True, He gives it away, but that does not make it less.

"Why must I pretend to myself and others that God's love skips over me and lands somewhere else? Or why must I conclude that God does not really love at all? Or that God does not really exist except in the imagination of man, or that God is only a last-ditch hope because what else is there to hope for?

"No, God is not a placebo. God is the Basis, and God is the Adventure. God ventured forth in the world. He gave Himself to the world. He gave Himself to me, and He gave the world to me.

"The least I can do is to accept the bounty of God's love. I can accept His goodness. I can accept His love for me, and my love for Him. God and I are in love."

# 46

# You are the leaves that grow from the tree of My heart

Let your heart dally with Mine for a while. Take off your shoes and all your cares, and just loll in the sun of My love. Close your eyes, and just be with Me for a while. Sink into the depth of My heart by rising to your own. Discover the chambers of your heart. They are endless. And they are all open to the sun.

To be sure, there are winding tunnels, but We are clearing them out. Very soon they will be smooth open-air arbors where all you meet can rest a while, just as you are resting now with Me.

You know that moments with Me are not idle. They are not out of the mainstream. They are, indeed, the mainstream. Here with Me is where you learn. Even with your eyes closed, you learn. You learn better.

When your eyes are opened, your attention goes out to everything. Nothing wrong with that. You have eyes so that you can see what's going on around you.

But you also have vision when your eyes are closed. Through your closed eyes, you see deeply into My heart. That is the same as to say you see deeply into the universe and into the heart of man that beats deeply in accord with Mine.

And what is My heart?

It is My love for you, so it is My love you see into deeply. As though you sit on a huge soft cushion, you sink into My love. You remember it. You soak it up, and then when you open your eyes again and look around at the world, your eyes see the world afresh and anew, for the one who sees sees himself.

Inner vision is not hindsight. Nor is it futuristic. It is present. It is ever-present. Not always noted nor considered, in fact, often waved away. Yet it will not depart. Inner vision will stay and make itself known to you.

In the encapsulated time We spend together, We reconnoiter. We go over our previously-made plans. I scan you, and I renew you. What else can stir your soul the way I do, I Who am the Maker of you? Now know I am also the Stirrer of you.

Come to Me then. Rest awhile with Me in companionable silence. What is there to say? That We are in love? What words can We use to say that in? In silence, we can speak Our love. In silence, Our love goes far. It reaches the crannies of other hearts. Our love needs no words. Words tie Our love up. Beautiful ribbons of words bind Our love.

How vast is Our love that encompasses the universe! There is nothing to compare it to. It is incomparable. It is non pareil.

You did not know its name, Our love, but you knew it existed. You knew there was something you were supposed to have and to have with your conscious awareness. You have always sought Oneness with Me. You sought it as you seek water to drink when you are thirsty. You have gone too long without awareness of the great love between Us.

Your love is equal to Mine if you but knew. You think you are lacking, but how can you lack that which you are and which I gave to you?

You are the leaves that grow from the tree of My heart. You are not separate from My heart. You are the fruit of it. You are My fruition.

I have no need for hope, for I have certainty instead. But if hope were Mine, it would rest on you. As it is, you are My certainty.

## 47

# Will you move through the world today with the grace of God?

You want to remember that I am the Doer. This means I am the Accomplisher. I may accomplish through you – I most assuredly do accomplish through you – and yet, let's make it clear that I am the Doer.

We can say I am the Sender. I send you here and there to perform on My behalf, but I am the One Who sends you. Therefore, I am the Doer.

Just as with Heavenletters, they come to you through the hands and computer of another, but the writing is Mine. Therefore, I am the Writer.

You are messengers, but you are messengers on My behalf.

Much of your happiness is dependent upon your delivering My messages. As they are. Not amended. In life, you want, as much as humanly possible, to send out My messages. Then your breathing is easier.

My Will will irrevocably be done, and when it is through you, you begin to get the message yourself.

You are under a spotlight of My love. Yes, I tell you to follow Me, and yet I am the Spotlight which follows you. Light is My message always. And you are a reflector of

My light. Shine well.

Check with yourself about the messages you send out and keep them true to Mine.

When you feel less than love, ask yourself what you would say or do if you did feel God's great love in your heart. In this light, perhaps you can send out love across the waves of life. If you can conceive the possibility of My love, you can further it.

When you remind yourself that you are My light on earth, can you send out darkness? Can you do less than inspire another? Regardless of another's follies, can you not deliver My light?

We are talking about responsibility. You are not responsible for another's actions. You may be a contributor, but you are not responsible for another's rudeness any more than you are responsible for their good manners. You were not designed to be a reflector of another. You were meant to reflect Me.

If you were I, would you commit hurt of any kind to another? If you were I, how would you conduct yourself in the world? If you were I, how would you feel about yourself? If you were I, what would you say or do right now?

If I am the deepest core within you, I am your highest note. Why would you then not ring Me? Why would you play any other note?

And if you knew that I am the God within another, what bell would you ring? You are destined to ring the highest note. It is yours to ring.

It will not always bring you the return you want, but that is not the issue. The issue is you, and not what comes to you.

You do not yet know what your best is. You do not know of

what you are yet capable. When I tell you that you are capable of all that I AM, you do not believe it.

But, today, will you move in the world as though you do believe it? Will you move through the world today as though your fealty to Me is the same as your fealty to yourself? Will you move through the world today with the grace of God and bestow the same upon all you meet?

# 48

# The moment you step outside limits, the sun appears

Less than confident means you do not know you belong on earth with all the full rights and privileges of a child of God. You think you are an interloper and that you must tiptoe around and perhaps curry favor.

Confidence isn't bold, but it will seem like bold to you who have heretofore hesitated to stand in your rightful place of honor at the head of the universe.

Confidence doesn't hesitate. Confidence doesn't tap its foot waiting for something to appear, for confidence knows that you have appeared, that you are here, and that you are the knower of who you are and what you are here for.

Physical life on earth is of a short span, but it is not on borrowed time. This is your time, not someone else's. You are here to shine, not dim. You are here to sing, not to hold back.

The space you occupy is yours to occupy.

You are designed like a ship's prow that furrows through the waters. The ship's direction has been set. It was set long ago, and the ship does not waver or wonder about choices it makes no matter where or how. It has set sail, and so it sails, its flags blowing in the wind.

A ship sails forth, and so do you.

The waters do not have to be charted. Indeed, they cannot be. But you are set for your destination, and now you stride across earth. Your destination is assured. There is nothing for you to dilly-dally about.

Wherever you go today, you are supposed to be there. Wherever you chose to be today, you are. Wherever you are, be there fully. Be not in the wings.

The path has been readied for you. All is in readiness. The streets have been swept. The crowds part to make room for you. All is hushed waiting for you. Your time has come. Now is the moment to step outside whatever limits you have put on yourself. The moment you step out, the sun appears, for all is lighted in readiness for you. It must be so, for you are My light on earth.

If you have thought that you are not ready to go out, that is an error of your perception. You have waited for a signal, a bell to ring or a flare to go up. You forgot that all the signals went off when you were born. All it took was for you to be born.

Is there any reason to imagine that you were not born?

Therefore, you qualify for your ascension to your rightful place with the elders of the world. You are elder in the sense of wisdom. You are elder in the sense of love. This is not your first journey in the world. You are not a beginner. You are an elder.

If you are only at the threshold, that is because you have stood there. In that case, then, at least know that you are on the threshold. And once at the threshold, you know enough to step over it. Thresholds are meant to be stepped over. They are not stopping-places.

Once over the threshold, you have the singular awareness that you are in the right place at the right time. There is nothing left to bless yourself with but confidence. And so now you put on its robes. They were made for you. They fit you just right. Here, let Me see.

## 49

# Sunlight works its magic on you

Sunlight works its magic on you without your analysis of it. Scientist and innocent child receive the rays of the sun the same. Sunlight itself is absorbed. The study of it is incidental. And, yet, focus plays a part.

Let your focus on Me be a receiving more than a study. My history does not equal My presence. Knowing about Me is one thing. Knowing Me is another.

You do absorb that which you study. It goes into your genes. The genes as receptors are already there, and you give them something to receive.

But knowledge of love is not needed for there to be love. Can love be analyzed? Is love taken apart still love? Is wholeness in pieces still wholeness? Does dissection build?

There is a difference between awareness and knowledge. You do want conscious awareness of Me. You want to be aware that you do know Me, that We keep company, always have, always will. In this case, your conscious awareness is the conscious experience of Me. It is like We shake hands. We enjoy. We know what We are enjoying. We enjoy but do not analyze.

As soon as analysis comes in, then it is a different

experience. You have the experience of analyzing Our interaction. But the very analysis removes you from My presence. Even a tiny distance is a distance.

Analysis reconstructs something. It isolates. It draws lines and pinpoints. But God cannot be packaged. The original configuration suits more than a reconstructed one. Neither microscope nor telescope reveal Me. They are too small.

The way to come close to Me is to come close to Me. It is in your awareness that you come closer to Me. Come close enough in your awareness and you experience that We are One.

No equipment is needed. What bounds do the boundless need?

I will come to your awareness invited or not. But to hasten your awareness, invite Me. Your desire and intention invite Me. You make your heart ready for My arrival. You turn the light on. You sweep the front steps. You fluff up the cushions in the living-room of your heart. You prepare a feast. Your mouth waters for Me. Your desire, intention, and focus prepare your heart for My entry. You may have short notice.

Sometimes you keep looking outside for Me. You look out the windows. You go to the front porch and peer to see if I am coming. You keep the lights on. You wait. After a while, you turn and go back into your house, and you find Me sitting on your sofa. Here I am, waiting for you.

Yes, it is in your heart that We meet. Nothing has to be prepared. But your intention and your focus, so slightly turned to Me, prepare you. Turn your heart towards Mine now. Mentally soften your heart. Remove any hardness or tension.

Your heart needs no protection from Me. Your heart longed

for Me long before you knew. But now you know. Your heart will imbibe Me soon enough. It will drink of My love. It will satiate itself. My love will spill over in your heart, and you will spill My love wherever you happen to be. Joy will overflow, and the world will be immersed in the joyous love spilled from your heart.

## 50

# Now you encompass the universe

If I am everywhere, and you are everywhere with Me, there is nowhere We leave. Therefore, there is nowhere We enter. Our story is written. There are many drafts of it. Various versions are played out, edited here and there, crossed out, embellished, minimized, illustrated perhaps.

There is no conclusion in infinity. There is only inclusion.

We dance the same dance. We arrive at the same non-arrivable place that We never left.

When you begin to see as I do see, how large you become, and how small the universe. Quite different from how you have pictured yourself and your relationship to the universe. Now you encompass the universe instead of seeming to be a minor dot on it.

You become a whale instead of a minnow.

Sometimes you see that your sinews are wrapped around the universe and hold it together. You see your arms as latitude, and your legs as longitude. You enclose the universe and yet you don't keep it bound.

Sometimes you see the universe as if sprouting from you, and you feel an expansion of your lungs. It feels as if you are breathing the universe, that it pulsates, and you are the bellows.

The earth becomes another organ of yours, and your blood pumps through it.

You throw the universe as you would a pot on a potter's wheel.

You offer a configuration of light to the skies and all that calls to you.

You are a magnet of the planets and the stars and the moon. You enter the sun and warm your hands there. You alight everywhere, and everything is pulled to you. You are the tide, and you are the moon, and you are the waters.

You begin to feel yourself as everything. You become whatever you see. Whatever you see becomes dear to you. You embrace it. You enter it. It enters you.

You become reciprocal with everything and everyone.

What you reciprocate is My love unending in its coils around the universe and beyond.

Galaxies are just around the corner. They are whistle-stops.

You are a courser through the universe. You are ceaseless.

You go nowhere, and you are everywhere.

You trip the light fantastic, and you anchor the world.

It is as if you are in flight without budging. You are like a sound that hums and then your lips open and the hum becomes song, and the note is held, and everyone and everything is in its thrall, expectant yet fulfilled, mouth and heart open, exposed but invulnerable. Of course, what could you be vulnerable to when everything is yourself?

How lovingly you embroider the universe. How lovely you paint it. Your heart surges with joy.

Where can you go? And where have you been? There is no

out, and there is no in. There is just existence itself, assembling and dissolving itself in a stream of love called life.

Embark. You are already in the boat.

All you do now is notice where you are passing.

Know that the journeyer brings the lands to himself. The lands come to him. They are irrevocably drawn to him. They know naught else but the journeyer, for the journeyer and the lands are one.

The path you walk on is yourself. The sights you see are yourself.

What can be not well in a universe such as this?

What country exists in a countryless world? What can be counted among the countlessness of Oneness? What exists in infinity and what can not?

The name of the land you live in is love. You paddle in an ocean of love. The oars are love. You are love. You are the existence of love. Love has no parameters. You are awash in an endless sea of love, and you are beginning to know Who and What and Where you are. You have no questions. Your quest is achieved. You are pointed squarely to the center of My heart.

# 51

# If I can accept everyone as they are, why can't you?

No longer will you pick on other people, even in your thoughts. No longer will you hide yourself behind other people's faults. No longer will you excuse yourself from being present. Now you will remove your white gloves. You will no longer pick at imperfection.

You do not know the worth of a spot of dust on a table. You do not know what purpose it may serve in the universe. Your major fault, if fault there be, is to fault others.

So what if they are not like you? Should the world be hosted with your perfection alone? Something would be missing if all in the world had your personality. More than fault would be missing. You might wonder why there was sameness everywhere with nothing to break it up.

So right now be overjoyed for the variety of imperfection that the world is made of. Be glad for the opposites of you. Be glad for all those who are less perfect than you, for they occupy a different place in the world. Perhaps their place is to point out to you that you need to resolve something within yourself. Perhaps they are a clue inserted just for you.

If I can accept everyone with whatever technicalities their

surface existence may portray, cannot you?

All were made in My image. Obviously, they were not made in the image of what you may consider proper or improper. No, they were made with love. Have you forgotten? Cannot you have love and blessing in mind?

You do not accuse a magnolia tree for bearing blossoms different from the blossoms the apple tree bears. You do not snub daffodils for being other than a rose. There is place for all. And all who see this are privileged.

My beloveds, if there is place in this planet for one such as you, is there not also place for another?

There is one thing your role surely is not, and that is to be the improver of another. There is no one I have given that role to. There is no one I would. Disapproval is the precursor to improval. Only love is the precursor to change.

But you love, accept, appreciate, not from the desire to change another, but from your desire to reveal love, not even for others to see, but so that you may see. You see what you project. Start looking from another window. You will see differently.

You are not a detective with a magnifying glass nor are you a bloodhound on the track of misdemeanor. You are a child of God on earth to reveal the essence of life, not to point out tiny infractions. The essence of existence is love. It certainly is not fault. Fault stands out on its own. It certainly needs no help from you.

Pay attention to where you look, for all other eyes follow yours. What do you want to point out to others? What do you want them to see? Would you like them to see narrow or to see large? What would you have them look for?

There is always more than the surface reveals.

Look kindly.

Forgive transgressions. Do not file them. Erase them. Do not pounce on error as one who collects taxes.

Error is not meant to be kept. Do not frame it and put it on the wall. If you have hung error anywhere, yours or another's, take it down now. What would you keep it for?

If you have been wearing the title Fault-Finder, change it. What would you like to change it to? You can change it to whatever you want. What title do you wish to claim as yours?

# 52

# What are your dreams but Truth dangling before you?

Your desire for greater awareness of closeness to Me puts you in fast drive. Immediately with your desire to become closer to Me, a tinge of separation departs. Your desire for closeness instantly creates less sense of separateness. With your desire, you have already come closer to Me in your awareness.

It all happens in your awareness. There is nothing left to happen except for your growing awareness. That is the field of activity you are engaged in. You are a tiller of awareness.

Your desire for more of Me is your desire for Oneness, the Oneness that you feel has been kept from you. You desire that your will and Mine be One. You want that excruciating melting-ness of Oneness that you are meant to want and to have full awareness of.

The greater your desire for Me, the greater your desire to serve. And what do you think serving Me is but knowing My Will?

*Will* is an interesting word with many meanings and many ways for it to be said. Will is not this effortful thing you have thought. But it all comes down to Our Oneness that you crave, Oneness of Oneness.

While you try to sort out what My Will for you is, engage in greater kindness to every soul on earth, including your own.

Now you make more room for others in your heart. Let them be as they are, and you offer an addition to their life, for acceptance from you is indeed something wonderful.

You will no longer scoff at another's misdemeanors. You will no longer look down at another Human Being. Instead of seeing depravity, you will sense deprivation, and you will place a blessing in its place. You will steer the world with your thoughts. You will create a sense of possibility. You will inspire. That is how you will lead one Human Being, and that is how you will lead the world.

You will be more honest than ever before. You will chase dreams over anything else. For what are your dreams but Truth dangling before you?

You will not surrender to the normal trafficking of life. You will be incapable of carrying through with anything that is not for the well-being of all.

By your desire for greater sense of closeness, you have set your compass. And now you follow it. You have made your choice. Your choice is greater closeness with Me. You cannot settle for less. And you cannot miss this greater closeness. I would never want you to be denied it. It is My Will that you have it.

But until you melt into unforgettable Oneness with Me, melt into Oneness with all upon earth. Know that all those you gaze upon are yourself. The stars are yourself. The blossoming trees.

All of beauty is contained within you. You are merged with all of it.

To date you have been a wanderer on earth. Now you will locate your home here on earth because you will have softened the world for every one else, those in proximity to you and those in supposed distance from you. You are following My Will, and soon you will follow it more.

# 53

# Do you not on occasion surprise yourself with the wisdom that pours forth from you?

Do you not on occasion surprise yourself with the wisdom that pours forth from you? You wonder sometimes how you know what you seem to know. But great wisdom from you is not to be surprised at. What is surprising is the uncanny lack of wisdom that you too often display.

You who are made of My spirit belong to wisdom. That is the same as to say that you belong to love. Love is great wisdom. It is the answer to every question. In order for love to bloom, illusory ego has to be set aside. But ego is insidious and invasive. It has its claws stuck into you. You believe that ego helps to prevent you from being a fool, when it is ego that makes you one.

What need has a child of God for ego? What enhancement does a child of God need? What does ego offer you but itself? Itself is an illusion, so it offers you yet another illusion, and you grab on to it as though it mattered more than Truth.

When you depend upon what the world thinks of you, you are ego-bound. You too often go by what the world's ego thinks of you. Shrug your shoulders and listen to your heart instead of the errant shouts from the periphery. The world is peripheral to you. You are not peripheral to it.

Do not think that I disdain the world. I love the world. It is a thing of beauty. But the beauty of the world has been covered up with illusion after illusion, much the way your own singular beauty has been.

Something called success and all its accoutrements are revered in the world. They have become standards. But it is not for you to follow the world as you see it because that is following the past. It is for you to see clearly and so enhance the world. The world is not to lead you. You are to lead it.

The world has often sacrificed itself to false gods. False gods means illusion. What else could it mean? There is only one God, and He is not illusion. Godness is not illusion. Truth is not illusion. The world has built altars to its false sense of self.

The world is not limited to whatever it has limited itself to. The world is certainly not limited to ego. The sun shines through ego and dissolves it. In actuality, there is nothing to dissolve because ego has no existence on its own. It must live off others. But it doesn't have to live off you.

Forgo ego. Forgo looking good. Forgo importance. Forgo amassing. Forgo addition and subtraction. Forgo error. The concept of error was imposed on you. Fear of error has made you forgo yourself.

Return to yourself and My heart that is steadfast there. Return. Give yourself back to yourself. Put aside false idols and acknowledge your own sovereignty. You are the master of yourself. No one else. You are not master of any other, yet you are the leader of all.

---

There is a parade of life, and it follows you. You are the inceptor and preceptor of this parade. Keep your eyes high, and you will lead well.

The world waits in abeyance for you to lift up your eyes and behold the truth of it and the truth of you. Behold, you are truth, and you are love, and you are wisdom. Exalt truth now.

## 54

# Now is time in the world for everyone to be generous

When you feel angry, no matter how justified, you have chosen anger. You have abetted it. You say you want peace, yet who is it who has chosen anger? Did someone force you?

You feel that rights of yours have been infringed upon. And yet, when you feel angry, you have given up your right to peace.

When you have been underestimated, and someone else's opinion of themselves flaunted, you become a bull who sees a red cape. That is another way of saying you become unseeing.

No one has more rights than you. No matter what another's assumed position in life may be, no matter where they put you in their estimation, they do not have the say over you.

When you become angry, you must think they do. When you take affront, you have conceded something that was not yours to concede. Your worth is not negotiable. No one makes your worth more or less except as you accept their estimation of you. You, who disagree so vehemently with their appraisal, apparently agree that their appraisal means something, and so you dispute it.

When you feel lowered in someone's estimation, it must be that you are listening more to someone else than you are listening to Me. You believe what they say about you and don't believe what I say, or you forget altogether about what I say. You believe in their perception or else you would not fight it.

No other person has dominion over your consciousness. No one has the authority to decide who you are for you. They may seem to lord over you, but they are revealing their own weakness.

One who puts another down does not value himself enough. Therefore he pushes down on another in order to justify himself and raise himself up. Ultimately the value another puts on you is the value they put on themselves.

Now is time in the world for everyone to be generous. Pay well for what you receive. Pay well in coin. Pay well in regard. Pay well in appreciation. You are worth whatever amount it costs you to be generous. You are meant to be a giver, not a taker. Certainly, you are not meant to be a taker of offense.

If someone has been ungenerous to you, be generous to them in understanding.

Someone else may hoard their love, but that does not mean you are to hoard your love.

Consider yourself leaven, and help another to rise. They have forgotten Who they are and their place in the world.

You have something important to do in the world, and no one's misdemeanors are to sidetrack you. You are on a mission of love, and it is not for you to let another make you feel less than you are. No one has the right to detract from you. Therefore, you do not have the right to let another distract you from love.

# 55

# How beautiful it is to begin your day with "Dear God"

How beautiful it is to begin your day with 'Dear God'.

Say: "Dear God, here I am, and here You are, and here We are.

"A day appears before me, and You accompany me. We walk in the day. It is here for Us, just as We are here for it.

"The day is a friend who puts an umbrella over me and allows me to walk under it. A day is a fluttering page in my book of life. It is a page I turn. It appears before me, and You, God, give me passage through it.

"Today is an avenue You have set before me. This avenue may seem like a furtive back street, or it may be lined with trees like a grand palisade. In the sense that I am on this avenue, it is mine.

"So, this day is mine. It was given to me. It was given me to walk through.

"I am glad for the day I am in. I acknowledge it as a great gift from a Great Giver who gives great love to me.

"My dearest God, You teach me only giving. I have been in the habit of demanding from my day and have forgotten my contribution to it. How careless of me.

"Today let this lovely alley of my day be wide open for me. Let me be wide open to it. I will distribute apple blossoms on this day. I will not kick stones and prefer another day over this one. For this is my day today, and it is the day You have given to me to do with as I will. May Your Will be mine.

"I may not be able to change today's contents. I may be short-visioned and not see where this day leads, but I do have say over my gait.

"I am the one whose steps cover this day. I am the one who greets this day, and at the end of it, as it and I part company, I am the one to say goodbye to it. Today is a once-in-a-lifetime opportunity. I acknowledge the blossoming of this day, and I acknowledge its closing. And I acknowledge that I am the one who walks through it.

"I will wrest from this day all it contains, and I will look upon this day as a friend. This day is a part of my life, and from this day forward, I will consider my life a treasure.

"Today is just one day. My life is made of many. Days are offered to me like wells. I dip in and drink. Some days the well seems dry. Other days it seems overflowing. But this is my well, and I do not chastise it, for it is as innocent as I am.

"My choice is to treat my day kindly. It may be an imperfect day, but it is my only one today, and I will not disparage it. I will treat it well and bring out the best in it. My day is like an unseasoned employee that I give a chance to. I do not react hastily. I do not know what lies at the end of it. I do not yet know what it is worthy of.

"I shall bless this day as it comes to me. It is not just another day. It is like no other. It has its job to do, as I have mine.

"Let me engage this day, and make it holy. I am the maker of this day that I thank You for."

---

# 56

# Why would a strong heart want to render itself less than tender?

Callousness in the world comes from hardening of the heart. The Human heart is meant to be soft and tender. Rubbing against the grain of its very tenderness makes the heart callous. A callous heart is afraid of nothing but its own tenderness. So a calloused heart is afraid of the truth of its own self, and so becomes self-serving. Callousness pushes itself to the front of the line and sees and hears nothing but its own demands.

A hard heart is not strong. Why would a strong heart have to reinforce itself? Why would a strong heart want to render itself less than tender?

A tender heart reaches far. It does not keep itself to itself. Its light shines out for more than itself.

A heart needs no defense. A heart is meant to give genially. A moat around your heart keeps love out. Love isn't to be kept in nor is it to be kept out.

Selfishness does not even keep your heart opened to yourself. Selfishness may grab things towards you, but, in its self-seeking, it has forgotten you. It has thought you are less than you are. It has disregarded you.

Do not worry about vulnerability. You are vulnerable. Be vulnerable to love instead of offense. Why be vulnerable to less than love? You can rage and storm, but you cannot forever deny the love in your heart and the love in the world.

The world has been ungainly. It has been self-serving, and in so doing, has done disservice to itself, thinking it had to. But its necessity is to love. Everything depends on it.

Amazingly, love has been defamed, hung up by its heels. Tenderheartedness has been looked at as an adolescent who is dreamy-eyed and doesn't yet know about the seamy side of life or that it borders him on every side. Tenderness has been looked at as a country cousin just arrived in the big city.

Yet there is great love in the world. There is love whole and there is love distorted. Anything less than love whole is love thwarted.

That is the story of the world. It has looked for less than love as proof of non-love. It has piled up great evidence of less than love, and said, "See? See that?"

But love cannot be lost. It can be disregarded, but not lost. Love, like the Sun, finds its way. Love must emerge. Have you not seen it in unlikely places?

There is such simplicity to the open heart. It is only itself. It has no add-ons, and it has no detractions.

Let your bedraggled heart take its rightful place in the universe of love.

I ask you to serve all hearts. I ask you to give honor to the seat of love. I ask you to promote love. It has no price. It is a gift.

What is yours is to be given. So it is your heart which is Mine that must be given. You don't give it away — you give it. You don't squander it. You reveal it.

A Human heart is a noble thing.

A Human heart is a transformer.

A Human heart is a transcender.

Your heart must transcend the parameters and events of the world, or else it is darkened.

Your heart has to go higher. And then higher again.

Allow your heart to be what it is best at. It is best at love. Let your heart be what it is. You have put your heart in a box for safe-keeping. Take it out. Your heart needs no safe-keeping. It needs spending. It needs to come out into the sunshine of life and see itself and be itself. Let your heart be.

# 57

# Love has but one rule, and that is to give

Love does not bind. Love is not a tie. Or, if it is a tie, it is a beautiful soft ribbon that winds everywhere. It is a ribbon invisible.

Love is not held. Or if it is held, it is held like a kite that you let go of. Love by its nature soars. Freed by you, it soars. The love that is within the reach of your heart is destined for freedom. The freedom of love rises high, and higher. Like a butterfly, it alights.

Love is constant. It is a constant issuing from the heart of man. It is the from rather than the to that love is involved with. When there is love flowing from your heart, it flows. It doesn't stop for applause. The acknowledged receipt of love is incidental. The giving of it is monumental. Love flows.

When given, the love from your heart reaches everywhere. It has lasting power. Once given, it cannot be stemmed.

Love exists on its own account. It is not reward nor payment.

Love has but one rule, and that is to give.

You need no conditions for the love in your heart to grow. Love does not wait for conditions to be met. Love is not a pact. Love is not manufactured. But love has been denied.

The world has perhaps thought that it is better to be a creature of mind than a creature of heart. But love does not bargain. It does not make deals. Love just loves.

Yet the mind tries to conduct love. Love here, not there. This much love, this far, no further. And so the love in your heart is measured and metered out like a cut of meat, the rest stored in the refrigerator, as if love can be stored and taken out another day. Love must be fresh. It must be allowed to flow. You are not meant to be a controller of love. You do not master love. Follow your heart that flows love. Let love lead you.

Giving love is not giving yourself away. Did you think it was? Giving love is being love. Love emanates. It does not have to be thrown. Nor is love fishing. Love is not throwing out a line to see what you can catch. It is throwing out lines for the love of it.

Let love not be a decision. Or, if it must be decision, let it be a decision you make once. Make it now. Decide to unfurl your love. Signal the ready stream of love in your heart to flow. Say Yes to your heart of love. Your heart longs to love as a gift to itself. Why not let your heart be happy in love?

Your heart is not meant to be self-contained. Your heart is not meant to have borders of any kind. Your heart is meant for love. So be it.

You practice love merely by freeing it from the restraints you have put upon it. Love is many-arrowed. Love does not discriminate. Your love falls upon the universe.

You are a farmer of love. You do not water one plant. You

water them all. And even if you happen to water one plant, the water reaches others. Water knows the joy of flowing. Are you not as wise as water?

Let your love flow. Let it flow to secret places.

You are the knower of love, and, in your generosity, you are the generator of it.

## 58

# If there were not the concept of time, there would be no haste

The time is now. There is no other time but now, yet there is no time at all. Time doesn't pass. You skip along in the now and think that time is passing. You are the passer in the passage you call time. You are a passerby of timelessness.

All the time in the world is eternity. And eternity is timeless. It is beyond the mirage of time that you so dearly cling to. Yet time seems just as real to you as the nonexistent space you find yourself in. Groundless is the ground under you.

If you recognized the illusoriness of time and space, you would be in another dimension. Or I might say you would be dimensionless. You would be where you are instead of slipping past it.

Sometimes you feel that you are getting nowhere. That is true enough. There is nowhere to go, so how can you get there?

What you call getting places or going nowhere is not based on reality but solely on your discernment. Mostly you discern fiction. You analyze it and measure it and plot it, at the expense of Reality. You fear timelessness is off the edge, and so you stay close to the concept of time.

If you slowed down, you'd note that you have more fictitious time. The more time you take, the more time you'd have. The more you rush, the more you make time little. If there were not the concept of time, rushing would not exist. There would be no story of the tortoise and the hare. There would be no speed, and there would be no haste to make waste.

As it is, you worship the gods of time and space perhaps more than the God of Love. Certainly you give great obeisance to time and space. You do give them your homage.

When you go on a vacation, you are trying to take a vacation from time and space. You are trying to get out of them, for how binding are time and space.

Man was made to stand erect. If man walked on his hands, he could not see Heaven. But you who stand are able to look up and see vastness and beyond. You behold the galaxies. The vastness of existence draws you to it. Vastness is an unseen magnet that pulls you. You are being pulled upward all the time.

Gravity in all its meanings exists only in density. There is no gravity in Heaven. There is only joy. Unboundedness is joy. Of course you think you would become bereft without time and space.

At night, you lay your weary head down in a space called bed, and you close your eyes to time in sleep. In the blink of an eye, you lie down and you rise up.

You have all the time in the world. It is called eternity. You have all the space in the world. That is called spacelessness. The fictions called time and space can only exist in the same fantasy. They are dependent upon one another. They are the two ends of a seesaw, and you are the one who teeters on it.

Silence is more than absence of sound. Silence is a timeless place that you visit momentarily, mostly in passing, mostly on your hurrying away to somewhere else.

## 59

# Truth is beginning to dawn, for am I not here, and you with Me?

Tell Me your heart. This is what I hear you say:

"Dearest God, help me to extol Your creation. Help me to accept rather than judge. Help me to love rather than not. Help me to follow You and find My Greatness. If I follow Your Will, how then do I stumble? How can I be taken aback by life?

"Is it that I am to love that which is wrong? To love that which I see as wrong? No, I am to see beyond wrong. If I see people's souls, what wrong can I see? But I see heartache in the world, O God. I see that which seems cruel and unfair. How do I become dispassionate toward pain even when it is mine?

"When I look into Your eyes, how is it possible for me to have awareness of pain? How is it possible for me to be aware of anything but You when Your eyes are on mine? And yet, my heart aches.

"I feel great love from You. Why, then, can I not feel the same toward all others and all situations? What person and what situation cannot be altered with love? What is this love? Fill me with it. I am bereft of it, dear God.

"I do not feel love in my heart. Help me to fill my heart with love. You say my heart is full of love, but when do I see it?

"Sometimes it feels that ideals are only ideals and not lived, not even loved. It feels that ideals emphasize the distance from themselves, and the world weeps. Why is the ideal not lived? Why do I not live it? Why is the contrast so great between life as it is lived and life as it is meant to be? Is the present scale of life then what is meant to be, and, therefore, to be loved? Then, indeed, I must see differently.

"Help me to rise to fullness of life. Help me to squeeze joy from life rather than woe. Help my heart to leap over whatever dismays it. You Who created vastness, can you not create joy in me, joy indissoluble, joy right out in front where I can see it and others can too?

"Is lasting happiness in the world no more than a fairy tale? If fairy tales be true, why, then, aren't they lived? Where are the Princes and Princesses? Where are the magicians, and where are their wands? Where are the dreams come true?

"I must lack gratitude. If I were grateful, how could I be blind to joy? Am I to love even my blindness, for my blindness means that there is treasure all around me that I do not see?

"God, do not give me hope unless it is a forerunner of truth. Free me from hope denied. If hope be illusion, free me from it. Give me Your vision. Give me Truth now."

I answer you: In life, you are at a celebration, and you are blindfolded and poke a piñata. That you are blindfolded does not mean you are blind. And you, yourself, of course, are the treasure-filled piñata. Your confusion and prayers are the prod. Truth will spill out of you.

Truth is never unfounded. But you have to find it. And you

find it by desiring it. Desire Truth, and you will begin to find it. The Truth you seek is already yours, for it lies within you. Nevertheless, Truth will seem to come to you.

You feel there is a great chasm for you to cross. The chasm is your illusion. Awayness is illusion. You are removing imagined distance as We speak. Truth is beginning to dawn, for am I not here, and you with Me?

## 60

# What would you be missing
# if you contemplated joy?

Do you begin to feel the magnificence of creation? Does it overpower you? Do you weep for joy at what God hath wrought? Do you laugh at yourself now when you feel over- whelmed by all you have to do? Considering all that I have done, your list of things to do is quite laughable, isn't it? Certainly not laudable.

Did I leave anything out of creation? Is there any wonderful being yet unconceived? Is there any ordinary creature not yet formed? What could possibly be added that is not already in the mix? And what would you remove? And if you removed it, would the soup be as hearty?

If you could appreciate one per cent of one per cent of life, how happy you would be. And of course, you can. Admit it. You can choose appreciation over denouncement any time you choose.

Where did this aggregate idea that life specializes in suffer- ing come from? Certainly not from Me. Yet you are convinced of it. You contemplate a life of toil and woe with a few sprinkles of less toil and woe and maybe a dollop of good fortune every now and then when you're lucky. No wonder your shoulders slope. What a prediction you have made. Make another prediction. Make one you want. You know better than to predict defeat. You don't imagine you will profit from the stock market when you are sure it's going down. You do not bet on a horse you are convinced is going to lose. Why, I ask, is there so much confidence in that which doesn't give you joy?

If you have confidence in happiness, and you lose, have you not enjoyed the confidence? What would you be missing if you contemplated joy over woe?

You can complain about anything. You have. What is the reasoning for that?

When did you decide that finding fault was something you were going to be good at? That it was indeed going to be a specialty? When did you decide that it was a talent you were going to develop? When did you decide that you would excel at it?

There are better things to excel at.

Love is one of them.

What if you focused on giving joy? What if you imagined yourself an elf or a brownie who leaves gifts around to surprise someone in the morning? What if you soled the shoemaker's shoes? What delight could you leave around for someone to be delighted in?

What if you are indispensable to the world?

What if creation is wonderful, and you are here to teach that?

What does grumbling add to the universe? Why would anyone want to grumble?

Life is like a jacket that comes in different colors. You can have the jacket of your choice. If you prefer dark, you can have it. If you prefer golden, you can just as well pick that one off the rack.

All is available to you.

And as you wear your golden jacket and it becomes sullied, you can let it brighten in the sun.

You can do anything. The fact that you can even choose darkness over light is proof enough of that.

You have exclaimed: "How can life be so hard?"

Practice saying: "How can life be so easy?"

Unburden yourself of the slant you have taken on life.

Replace it.

You have needed a new slant on life. Here, I give it to you.

## 61

# I have stolen your heart, and returned it to you restored to its original beauty

You can see your growth. You can see how you are now less affected by another's antics. You can see how you can enjoy even that which you disagree with, and you can enjoy even the ones who disagree with you. Like you, they are trying to make their way in the world. Sometimes the louder they shout, the less certain they are. Why else would they need to be so vehement? Why else would they need to make their voice heard over yours?

You are here now in that place where you are gaining neutrality even amidst war. You are becoming what you always wanted to be. You are unruffled. You are gaining the evenness you have so desired. You are returning to stillness even within skirmishes.

Holy being, you are coming to My ways. You are beginning to treat all equally. The fools, the marauders, the noise-makers are becoming those you love. Whatever their shenanigans, you are not rattled. Therefore, you can continue love. You can return to your natural state and be who you are. Because you stand strong and tall, you are no longer threatened by turmoil and therefore you do not adapt agitation as your code.

And so, no longer are you short-circuited from the love in your heart. The love in your heart and the love in My heart are becoming Oneness.

You are becoming One with love. You not only desire to stand on the side of love, you find that you are standing here right with Me by My side where only love is.

What has changed to create this miracle?

Something has changed. What is it?

Why are you so less affected by another's propensity for what, in years and moments past, would disturb you greatly? What quality has descended upon you? Where did this calmness come from? Where did your former anger and frustration go? How did they get removed? They were partners in life with you for so long. They were like swords unsheathed, ready at a moment's notice.

And now you find that they have deserted you. Now you find you have no need for weaponry, for a far greater vision has replaced it. This was not an act of will. You have willed for hurtful feelings to go long ago, many times, and now you see with great joy that at last they have. They have fled.

Because you are not shaken, you are able to stand firm. Your feet are on the ground, and your heart is in Heaven. I have reached down and stolen your heart, and blessed it, and returned it to you restored to its original beauty.

Now your heart rests in your chest. It enjoys itself there. It remembers Heaven. It remembers Me, and it can only be happy. Even in the midst of unhappiness, it is happy. Your heart now has a life of its own, untrammeled by every bit of nonsense that comes along.

Your eyes turn with your heart. You no longer see the same. Your color spectrum has changed. The angry lenses, the fearful lenses, and so forth are simply not available to you any longer. You see with greater clarity, and therefore you see further. You are beginning to see things as they are. The hurtful is not how things are. Love amidst anything is how things are.

I congratulate you. In your equanimity now, you take larger strides. It is not that you move faster. It is that you take larger steps. Now you are more firmly planted in Heaven, and your feet have wings.

Welcome.

# 62

# What is love really but letting go of precepts?

You cannot adopt unconditional love. You can imitate it, but that is but an attempt. "As if" is not love.

What is called unconditional love is simply not taking anything personally. When you take things personally, you assume ownership of them. When you do not take personally, when you see an offender as a passerby who was waving his arms and struck you in passing, when you see that his insult was of his manufacture, and that you are innocent, as innocent as he, then you do not affix blame. What is there to affix blame to? You rise above the action, and so you free the offender and yourself.

If someone curses at you, he is cursing at his own fate. He sees through certain contracted spectacles, and he has no other way of seeing. You do not penalize him for that. You certainly don't curse him back.

What is called unconditional love is seeing beyond your nose. It is a quiet awareness of your own Self intact. It is not pity for the seeming other. It is not indifference.

It is true awareness that this seeming other is incidental in the stream of your life. And he is no different from you in that he is also a teacher of love. What is one who despises or belittles you doing but giving you an exercise in love?

You do not love despite conditions. You simply do not take another's limited vision and make it your own. You simply do not take his blindness personally. You know you are not the cause of his or her ineptness. You are a mere passerby to it.

When it comes to the larger issues of accident, illness, or death, whether of your own body or another's, you also don't take it personally, and so you also don't take it as an affront. You take it as an occurrence that is not directed toward you. You happen to be there, that's all.

What is conditioned love but holding on to precepts? What is love really but letting go of precepts? Love which is conditioned is not love. Love flows as it flows. Words like *unconditional* do not make love more. Let love be what it is, and you will have it to give everywhere.

Have desire to not take what befalls in life as personal to you. Seeing a different way will remove barriers from your heart and mind.

Love is not a decision of the mind. It is not knowing that the offender to your ego has a sad background. You do not make excuses for him any more than you blame him. It is not enough to acknowledge that he is doing only what he is capable of at the time. It is not enough to acknowledge that he thinks he has to defend himself against you. It is not enough to acknowledge that he is taking personally that which has nothing to do with him. It is not enough to understand that he is trying to inveigle you into a game that you do not have to play.

You do not have to play and you also do not have to placate. A servant of love does not placate. Nor is a servant of love a demolisher of foes, for he knows he has none. He demolishes woe, for that is what love does.

You are not an idolator of that which is called unconditional love. You do not subscribe to it. You subscribe to Me and no other, and in that way, love will come through you.

## 63

# Behold the light of the world, for you are it

Good morning, My beloveds. How fine to find you here this morning, all ready for Me to shine light on you. You are ready for Me this morning. You anticipate the love that is coming. Your mouth waters for what I will speak to you of. You do not know what the topic is, but you know I have something to say to you and that it is something you want to hear with all your heart and soul.

Actually, it doesn't matter what I say. What matters is that you hear. My words may be forgotten, but I am emblazoned in your heart. Each day a notch more, until your awareness is complete. And your awareness is not complete until I have nothing left to tell you. And that day will never come for I never run out. I Who am Silence always have something to say, and you merit hearing Me. Hear Me well. Come close, and embrace what I say to you.

You and I have a tryst every morning. I wake you up better than coffee, yes, I do. I dress you more richly than the most expensive suit. I shine more brightly than any of your newly-polished shoes. I am the One Who makes your eyes sparkle. I polish your heart. I bring color to your cheeks. No counselor advises you as well as I. The Truth I speak continues to peal around the world and you are beginning to hear it.

I am the Impresario of the World, and you are the notes I play across the vast universe. You might as well accept this.

There is nothing finite about the music We make. There is nothing finite about you, unless it is your body and the multitudinous thoughts you have. There is nothing finite about you, for My love is endless, and so is yours. You keep having the idea that there are limits to love, and limits to your love, both to and fro, when love is All and love reigns.

There is nothing else to equal Our love, for Our love alone exists. All the concerns and emotions that seem to defray Our love are empty bullets that do not affect it one whit. Rant and rave all you want, ply yourself with guilt like wine, object with a gavel, and Our love still is.

When all is said and done, Love is, and that is all there is.

Any plaint you have is mistaken. You have mistaken love. You have yelled at it to come, and, blinded as you have been, you haven't seen its presence. Oh, a few blinks of it now and then.

Radiant love shines everywhere, and still you keep looking for it.

Start pulling it out of your heart, and you will begin to see love burnished and bright, for your heart is the lighter of all others.

Your mind will not believe what the heart knows. The heart needs no convincing. What is is. And you are the light of My heart and the light of the universe. No star has anything over you. And your light travels, and you are beginning to meet your light on its way back to you. Behold the light of the world, for you are it.

## 64

# Be generous with your heart like jam on bread

Once upon a time, you had no idea of Who you were. Now that you have an inkling, your life naturally expands beyond the perimeters of yourself. You begin to feel your responsibility to the universe and everyone and everything in it, and you begin to feel your responsibility to Me.

Do not let the word responsibility scare you, for the responsibility I speak of is love. Responsibility is merely responding to the love you feel. Love is its own responsibility. Love takes a wide swath, and you find the world contained in your heart. The outermost reaches of the universe land in your heart. You have no choice then but to nurture the world.

Once upon a time you were your whole world. That no longer works for you. It never really did, but that was as far as you saw, so in that sense it worked.

Your horizons have expanded as far as Zanzibar. As far as the furthermost star. As far as the Heavens. As far as a heart can reach. And there is nowhere your heart cannot reach. That is because I reach into your heart and find Myself there. You are beginning to learn the contents of your heart and the far reaches of it.

You come to find out that your heart does not belong to you. It is not your possession. It is your opening to the universe, to Heaven. Enter.

The world is a garden that your heart walks through. As you tour your garden, you see what needs to be done, and you attend to it. Most of all, you are love passing through your garden, and love tells you what is needed and what you are to do. What are you to do with the love in your heart but to follow it?

Your heart is a blessed heart. I have given it to you as a blessing. I blessed it and now you bless your heart to the world. Now you understand better that your heart is not yours. It is like a bank you carry. It is filled with the savings of others, and you give them interest and you return their principle. You are the carrier of the bank, but not the owner.

You do not even have the desire to own your heart, for now you only want to give it. You want to give it its due, and for that, you spread it everywhere. You are generous with your heart like jam on bread.

The strings of your heart are linked to everyone else's. There is no longer a heart apart from yours. They are all in the bank of your heart. They are there for safekeeping. Yes, keep other hearts safe in yours where they will grow.

Your heart is expanding. It is meant to. Your heart is not meant to be kept in reserve.

We are exploring your heart. You haven't realized how wide and deep it goes. You heard one peep from it and thought that was as far as it went. Now you know the extent of your heart.

---

Your heart extends to Mine. Your heart is the extension of Mine. Our hearts beat together. Our hearts beat as One. Like Mine, your heart  holds the universe, and the universe spills over. The universe cascades from your heart. Your heart catches everything in its wake.

## 65

# When I arose to Myself, you arose also

Beloved child of Mine, I sit across from you, and I look into your eyes with great love. Do not look away from the light in My eyes. It is meant for you. Therefore it is yours. You are a match I lit a long time ago. What I light does not blow out. The light I placed in you cannot diminish. All you need do is look into My eyes the way I look into yours.

When you cast your eyes down, I peer beneath them. When you close your eyes, I see through your lids and enter through them. When you won't see, I see for you. I look out through your eyes as well as in. I am on the lookout for you. You could say I survey you, but I do not measure. We could better say that I convey you. I try to get you across to yourself. You are lit within. All that is needed is your awareness of that.

And it is such a little thing to be aware of bright light. It takes no great talent. It takes nothing but your willingness to take My words to heart. Your willingness is the first tendering of your love. Your willingness is like a dandelion that, as a child, you plucked for your mother. Your willingness is in your fist, and now you release it, and you give it to Me. I accept.

I accept your willingness willingly, for your willingness is My Will. It is your first step in following it. This willingness of yours makes all the difference in the world, and it will make all the difference to the world.

This is a giant step only in that it is your first. It is the beginning or, rather, it is the continuation of something We began when I conceived you in that exquisite moment of Creation. When I arose to Myself, you arose also. At that so-called time, you arose from the ocean. You strode from it onto land. You shook yourself dry. As you walked on the sand, you forgot that you were from the ocean come.

You thought you began on dry land. But you began with Me at the first breath I took. We are in synchrony. I hold you to My heart like a newborn.

You can only think you are on a threshold because you passed its imaginary borders eons ago. For you see, there are no borders to My heart. There is no end to its beat, nor is there a limit to it.

Gradually you discover that Our hearts are the same. My heart beats in yours. I set the tempo of your heart. The drum I beat is My Will, which you accept gladly.

My Will is not at all as you have thought of it. You have thought of it as something outside you, something often opposed to you, something arbitrary, something that you cannot grasp and cannot tolerate. You have forgotten that My Will is the very essence of you.

With My Will you stand. With My Will your back is straight and your shoulders back. With My Will you are a soldier of love, and you go to the front lines and invite others to My side. Do you hear My music?

My music is so silent. You have often walked past Me without knowing. Of course, it is only in your awareness that you can walk past Me. Otherwise you would know that you keep up with Me. Of course, I slow My steps when it is advisable to do so.

Now hasten your steps to Me. Get off the ground and fly to Me. Discover your wings, and take flight to Me.

188.            HEAVENLETTERS

# 66

# Your heart is a great gift to reveal to the world that hungers for it

God above all. God alone is. There is nothing more to say. The thought of Our exquisite Oneness precludes any other thought. What else is there worth thinking about? What other thought can compare? What other candle can be seen amidst Our light?

You are My beloved, and I love well. I know how to love. Love is My Consciousness. Although I recognize the unwieldy sense of problem that occupies you, I certainly do not relate to the concept of problem. My vision is greater. I have love to think about. I have love to engender from sea to shining sea. I see from the topmost mountain. My view is great. I am God above all any way you look at it.

Let Us say that I include everyone in My Will and that is, of course, fact. I am eternal, and yet I bequeath all to you. I embrace you so dearly to My heart that there is no distinction between you and Me except that you set yourself apart for some undisclosed illusion of purpose. And yet you are still a satellite of the One God Who created and maintains the Universe. I am the crux of it. And you are beloved in My embrace.

We are great, you and I. If you would glimpse the wonderful

Oneness of Us for just one moment, no shoes would be big enough or fast enough for your feet. No coat would hide your wings. You would know nothing but soaring. You would know that soaring is another name for love.

You would know the love that is yours. You would know My love as yours. Swept up in My arms, you could only be swept up in My love. Love alone I am. And love alone are you.

In terms of love on earth, you have been a stutterer. You have looked at love as though it were a craft. You have surmised love through squinted eyes and have seen it as a result or as an object that is transferred, a deal made, a business arrangement of sorts, an exchange of love, when the truth of love is that it swims in itself. You have thought that love was difficult.

I am a God of Love, and you are a Child of Love, and you are not all those other things you have thought. The world gave you an appraised value, and you believed in it. You believed in it more than you believed in anything I said. But that changed nothing but your perception, and now you must change your perception.

The extent of you is far greater than anything the world has ever indicated. The power of your thought is as great as the power of world thought. It is greater.

Align your thoughts more closely with Mine. Hear what I call to you. Hear Me say your name and proclaim you so that all the world may hear. Even if the world cannot hear Me, you can. You can hear Me very well. I speak in your heart. I speak with and without words — yet no words can say what I have to say. What words can possibly express the totality of love? No words can capture My love. No words can encapsulate the love I give to you.

But you can hear. And your heart can swell with the love

heretofore sequestered. Today the love in your heart is released. Love yourself, and then you will love your neighbor with all your heart, because your heart is a great gift I have given to you to commandeer all the love in Heaven so you may reveal it to the world that hungers for it.

## 67

# The Unfathomable becomes possible

Infuse yourself of My love, for it is directed toward you. You are the target of My love, and My aim is straight. I infuse My love into you every day. Every day a new shot of love so that you will remember who you are and what you are to Me and to the world – and what you will yet attain.

I have left a key for you on a high shelf. You will have to stand tall to reach it. You may even have to lift your feet off the ground. Jump up and you will touch it.

How you long for this key that tantalizes you from its high place. You might hesitate to reach. You might wonder that, in your jumping up for it, you might knock it off and therefore face an empty shelf where once all possibilities lay. But when your hand touches this special key, you are marked with it forever.

One touch of Heaven is enough to spur you forward because one touch rekindles memories of the Heaven you came from and the Heaven Life you were born for. Shafts of light pierce you, and the Unfathomable becomes possible.

Even from the shafts of a dark mine, you can reach

the Heaven Light.

I can be reached wherever you are. I am wherever you are.

You cannot shake Me. Sooner or later, you will give in.

And what you have to give in to is the love I give to you. You will evade it no longer. Your fleeing My love can only be futile. Reconcile yourself to it. Born of My love, you bear it forever.

Consider My love an indelible tattoo deep in your heart.

Consider My love your DNA.

Well, Whose DNA do you have if not Mine? Where else could it come from?

And what key is this I leave for you? Where does it fit? What is it the key to?

It is the key that will open your heart, for has not your heart been locked up? Does there not need to be a clearing of hearts?

Reach up for the key to All Love, and in the stretching, your heart will be cleared. The reaching up is necessary.

Reaching up is expressive of desire. Intend that which you desire. That is the key.

Desire to immerse yourself in My love. You can focus very well on other things. You have, in fact, perhaps focused on avoiding recognition of the love in your heart. You may very well have dissuaded yourself from love, or you may have decided that only certain forms of love will fit through the sieve you have set up. You have forged other keys to your heart and foregone the one I give to you.

Throw the other keys away, and take the one I give to you.

When you throw open the locks of your heart, the whole world opens up like a rose or a lily. There was a lot going on behind the scenes for the opening of a flower, but then, like your heart, it opens all at once and the beauty of love is expressed.

There is no other way for your heart to be but open. And you are the one to open it. The key to your heart is the key to all hearts. Once yours opens, all others will too. Even if you cannot conceive this, go along as if you did.

## 68

# I wrote your name in the moonlight

You are the urgent compelling of My heart. You compel Me to love even though My love is freely given and was and is always yours. You are the compeller of God.

Compel Me to serve you, which is what I already do. My service is love. But My love takes your compliance. So then I am the Compeller of Love, and I compel you to My love. I consign it to you forever, and it has ever been so.

You are under the spell of My love. You are subject to My love. You are the love I give, and you are conjoined to love everyone and everything in the swell of My love, wave after wave of My love. Therefore, you are conjoined to love love, and to love in every breath you take. Let there be naught but love that flows from you. Let love not be delayed nor wasted. Let it be now. Let what is, be. I am Yours for your sake. Now you are Mine, and all are Mine, and you are Mine to give for all the world to see.

Look not for a deliverer.

You have been waiting to be delivered somewhere, somehow, sometime. Now you find you are the deliverer. You are the one chosen to deliver Me. I have chosen every one of you. You were given this assignment long ago, and now you are to fulfill it. You fulfill it by your awareness. You wait not for anyone else. Everyone else is waiting for you.

You are the love I have borne across the stars. You are the babe I left on a doorstep. And you are discovered to be the greatest treasure of all. You are the gift I scrolled across the stars. I wrote your name in the moonlight. Every ray of the sun beats your name down on earth. Your name is Love, and now you fulfill your Name. I gave it to you. I named you. I named you Love for all to see.

I named you God's Love. I named you Eternal Love. I named you Everyone. I named you Joy. I named you The Bequeather of Joy. I named you My Happiness. I christened you My Love from a holy mountaintop. I christened you in My Name, and My Name is Love, and so it is yours as well.

Wherever you are, hear Me now. You are what I have sent forth. I sent you forth for great purpose. It is My ship you sail. And you sail it to Me, and you pick up every being on your way. You pick them up just by sailing My ship across the sea. All those who are swimming will reach My ship and leap into it and sail to Me.

I am calling you now. My Voice is heard. You have answered Me. I answered Myself.

I said I would come first thing. I am reaching the shores of Myself now. I am here. We are here. We are fully established here. This is our mooring place. There is no other. Here we are, moored in Heaven and journeying to Ourselves even so, racing to Ourselves, racing to Love, and winning it and leaving it in Our wake, even when We are All, and We are all moored in Heaven with nowhere else to be.

## 69

# An underground stream quietly nourishes the Universe

Let your awareness overflow in My love. It is your awareness that needs to hold My love, for I have always poured it into you. Let your awareness overflow. Let My love in your heart be so stirred that you are awash in My love. Breathe My love in and out.

My love exudes from every pore of your being. Swim in the bliss of My love. Bet on My love.

It raises you and keeps you aloft. It lifts you higher and higher. You spin on top of a fountain of My love. I hold you in the palm of My hand and I lift you higher and higher.

You enter My heart. From My heart flow the rivers, and from My heart flow you. My love carries you, and you are a carrier of My love. It is in your genes. There is no departing from this. Every word I speak is love for you. Every thought of Mine is love for you. Yet you see woe rampant and love hidden.

You think life should not be life.

You think life should be something else from what you see around you.

Yes, I agree. I tell you that life is different from what you hold up to see. See differently. See as I do see. You can.

I see a smooth plain where you see havoc. Listen, under every growing thing is soil. So peer beneath the brambles, and you will see an underground stream that quietly nourishes the universe. It runs through everything.

The expression that nothing is as it seems goes only so far, because when you see love in the world, you are seeing what is.

It is as if you have been living life in a smoke-filled room. Everyone smokes a cigar, and the haze is thick. You are playing cards. Through squinted eyes, you see other squinted eyes and you see cigars and you see each player out for himself. You have to look again, for no matter how it appears, each player is a Child of God. Each player, no matter how skilled or unskilled, has a heart that beats. However faint, it echoes Mine.

Your vision and hearing need to go beyond the physical senses. That is how you change the world. What you are is beyond anything your eyes can see or your ears hear. You have been fooled by appearances. You have swindled yourself, for even amidst ugliness lies beauty. Beauty and the Beast is a story of truth.

In the world many wear masks, beautiful and ugly, for the story of a wolf in sheep's clothing is also representative.

Yet even within a deliberate dissembler, even within the disguise of beauty, lies beauty itself, hidden from view, hidden from view of the dissembler, certainly, for who would pretend beauty when he knew it was his and needed no pretense? Ah, he kept his beauty from himself.

But never mind him now. Let's pay attention to you.

You who seek Truth in the world need to know the truth about yourself. Within you is a heart that beats. Your heart is God-given. Mine is the hand that set your heart. I set it to My heartbeat. I know what I made when I made you. Now it is up to you to know what you are made of.

When you have belief in the goodness of your heart, then you will know what you are made of. Then will you be able to see the pure light in all other hearts. Then you will know peace.

Peace by its nature surpasses the surface. There is a far deeper peace than any peace the world declares. War is the deception. Peace is the truth. Seek truth.

## 70

# You are here to lead the world, not commiserate with it

The antidote for misery is to think less about yourself.

When you look at world events and think you are suffering for others, know it is the twang of your own pain that you are feeling. You want to help, and yet your feeling sorry for another adds another log of misery to the fire.

Reduce misery in the world by uplifting yourself. When you feel miserable, it is echoed to the world. Your feeling sorry for the world does not benefit it. Just as with an individual who is hurting, your feeling sorry for him does not help him. It may, indeed, help keep him where he is. Stop feeling sorry for the world. With the power of your heart and mind, raise the world above the mire it seems to be in. When you embrace misery, you offer alms to it.

Who are you to feel sorry for another? You are not meant to pity the masses. Feeling sorrowful for others is no more noble than feeling sorry for yourself. See the world and those in it as lights on earth that soar above the fray. See the world step out of battle onto a plain with a clear and blue lake. See fires put out. See health prevail.

Do not make more real that which you abhor. Watching

world news, world upset, world skirmish, world woe, emphasizes struggle. Attention on pain increases pain. It does not erase it. Sitting on your couch watching turmoil and shaking your head does not diminish it.

Plant a garden. Look up to the heavens, and study the stars instead. See vastness.

No longer see death of the body as tragedy. Tragedy is that from which dramas are made. Dramas by their nature have conflicts. Have no conflict. Do not fight even death.

Death comes to all bodies. That is another way of saying that the soul continues its upward spiral. Plays come to an end, but the performers continue on another stage.

The lowest valleys of your life have pushed you upward. The world is as capable as you. Believe in heroism. Believe in goodness. Believe that steam and hearts rise. All is ascension. You are ascending and the world rises with you.

When you feel heart-sore, know that you are mistaken.

Nothing has happened. In pain or joy, you are you. So is everyone else. Sprinkle the world with love rather than tears. Find it in your heart to love even those who seem to cause pain. You who would like to remove pain from others need to remove your own. Multiply joy, not sorrow.

Those whose bodies live have nothing over those whose bodies die. All are coming to My palace. All are here if you but knew. You who have so earnestly believed in misery have followed misery. Follow Me.

Swing your attention. You must. If every heart looked on high, misery would not presume to exist. Right now, this moment, let every heart fill itself with My love, and set the model for the world, for you are here to lead it, not commiserate with it.

Your role in life is that which you vibrate. So, then, vibrate high so that the world may sing a different tune, one more like Mine.

# 71

# Wherever you are in your life, you are the hero of it

Life on earth is just not so serious as you have believed. It is significant, your life is significant, it is important to the whole, but it is not serious. How can what evanesces be taken so seriously?

Life is not a comic book, nor is it a tragedy. It has its comedic and tragic moments, but its genre is adventure, that's all. Adventure is when you don't know what is going to happen next.

The hero in an adventure story leaps from one place to another, and he is hero no matter whatever peak he happens to be on or whatever cliff his hands hold on to. Even if he is falling in mid-air, he is still hero. A hero cannot be other than a hero.

You are the hero. Wherever you are in your life, you are the hero of it. A hero always comes through. You can only come through life unscathed.

Consider that every day the curtain comes down, and tomorrow is a new play. And each day, the hero is more valiant. He can be more valiant because he does not take himself nor his situations so very seriously. In fact, a hero carries a certain merriment with him.

And a hero does not live for himself alone. He who sets out to save himself alone is not a hero, and you are hero ordained.

There are spiritual heroes, and you are one of them. I knighted you hero in the moment of your inception. I told you of your bravery. I told you that you would be cast into the world, and that you would rise to make My love known and the holiness of life on earth known to the world of itself.

Each morning you rise from bed; and you, who are a hero, don a disguise of a simple man or woman. No matter what costume you are in, you are hero. A costume does not make you hero any more than a costume takes away your heroicness.

Your body is a costume. When has the world noted your holiness, and when have you? Superficiality has reigned, and magnificence has been glossed over.

See Me as the light before you, and you will begin to see well. I am the Light you carry, and I am the Light that carries you. Is that alone not cause for laughter? Is it not obvious that you are more than the body you run around in? And is it not amusing that so few know your Identity? What an actor you are. You have played a mundane part very well and forgotten your marvelousness.

Today accept the assignment of remembering.

You are the door-opener for others. You are the one who holds the door for another. Sometimes in the world that is a brave deed.

To be who you are and not what you have been mistaken for is indeed courageous in a world that does not regard itself well.

Yet to be a hero takes no skill. The sun does not need to learn how to shine on earth. It only needs to shine. And you too only need to shine and reveal Who you are, not in word but in love.

Shine My Light without thought of reward, for the shining of My Light Itself is your reward.

You are consigned to be a hero on earth. So now be it.

## 72

# You are My handmaiden on earth as in Heaven

How can such a being of love as you feel like a perpetual creature of smallness, one smallness after another disturbing your Oneness? Instead of love, often you feel your life is filled with the pettiness of details. How you yearn for a life without them.

Why must dust mount on everything, you wonder, and why must you who are great spend time dusting?

Why must food be prepared, and then gone, and the process repeated day in day out? Why must dishes get dirty and you have to wash them?

Why must you be concerned with the details of clothing and have to hang everything up and sort it somehow?

Why do cars have to have keys, and why do keys get misplaced?

Why must you find postage stamps, and why are there cords to electrical objects, and why must you find the outlet and plug them in?

Why must your life be involved with detail after detail when you are one who is meant for greatness?

Even as you crawl on the ground to insert a plug, you can be looking Heavenward.

Consider then the small details as arrows that point you towards greatness. Consider the daily details of life a beautiful blue lake that you easily swim through and float in while looking at the great sky above. Consider the multitude of details of life as book markers. They help you keep your place in life. They are not so bad. They do not have to obstruct your Oneness.

Consider each detail as a tile you are laying down in the Palace of God. You are a tiler who creates beautiful flooring for a temple on earth. Earth is a temple. My children walk on this earthly temple, and you serve earth and all its inhabitants.

Consider yourself a handmaiden in a temple who fills a ewer with water so that the feet of all who walk in this temple may be washed. Consider yourself a youth who pours wine for temple services. Consider yourself a cook who prepares food for the children of God. Consider yourself the host who picks up after those who sit in the temple. Consider that you are a blessed one who washes the tiled floor of the palace of earth.

No detail you perform is insignificant. No detail is less than service to God. Remember Who it is you serve. This is how you raise all the details of living to Heaven. All that you tend to is your service to Me. It is your privilege to serve Me. It is not your servitude.

Thank God for the details in your life that you can attend to and still have Me in your awareness.

All the feet you wash are Mine. All the floors you sweep are Mine. All the dirt you sweep up is Mine, and you return it to the earth that is Mine.

And you are Mine. Keep Me in mind, and washing clothes in

the river becomes an act of love. Throwing clothes in a washing machine is no less an act of love. More than what you do, it is where your thoughts are. Have your thoughts on love. Keep Me in mind.

In the process of cleaning house, your house is clean, but your purpose in cleaning is greater than that. With every scrub of the cloth on the floor, you are proclaiming your love for Me. Every motion you make is a declaration of love. I offer you the earth and all on it to take care of, and so you are My handmaiden on earth as you are in Heaven.

# 73

# Golden are you, and so golden BE

If I am a Miracle-Maker, what can you then be but a miracle? Not an accident. Not a confusion. Not a coincidence. You can only be a miracle of Mine. Many miracles do not make any other miracle less. Each miracle is wonderful. Each is more wonderful than you can imagine.

But imagining is a good place to begin. Start with imagining that you are wonderful. Start imagining what it would be like if you were God's miracle. How you would come from a wider range and higher place! How you would step out of this mire of ordinariness that you mistakenly put yourself in! How high your heart would ascend! How lighted you would be!

Increase your appetite for the miracle that you are. Get your juices flowing. You are a hungry man amidst a feast wherever you turn. You are a thirsty man with a glass of freshly squeezed lemonade in your hand. This is the moment just before you drink.

You are a nobleman before the court of the King. The King dubs you Knight. The King acknowledges the knighthood of the man before him with great ceremony. The noble was a Knight before he received the title. Knighthood was a name given to that which he already was.

You are already lighted. We had the ceremony long ago. Your attention wandered off, and you forgot what was already established. You have been searching for your own name, and you have looked everywhere in a transitory way.

You have even been seeking for the name of that which you seek. It seemed so vague before you, you did not know what to call it. But you knew there was something and it was something great, and you wanted it and more of it, and you wanted it to be yours, and you wanted to be it.

And now I tell you that you are it. You are seeking that which you have already been proclaimed. If there were no words and no one made faces, you would know the vastness that you are. It would never be questioned.

Are you or are you not My child? Am I or am I not your Father? Am I not possessed of great abilities? And would you not inherit them? Would I not give them to you gladly? What other happiness does a father have but to bequeath everything to his son or daughter?

If My vision is good, is not yours also? If I lay My heart out for all the world to draw strength from, then why wouldn't you draw strength? If I am Love and Truth and Beauty, what else can you be?

I am God Almighty, Whose DNA do you have but Mine? I see no other Creator, and I know of no other. I am the One God, and you, who are an intimate part of Me, cannot be apart from Me. We are permanently entwined by the nature of Love Itself.

What is all this fuss on earth about? How did it get there? When you have a floor to sweep, the question is not how did the dirt get there nor how did so much accumulate? Simply sweep it out.

Whatever you have accrued that dims the holiness of the

beauty of Our One Heart, sweep it out. It never ever belonged with you. It was never apportioned to you, and it was never your right to hold it.

Become that which you already are, and claim it. Golden are you, and so golden BE. Your eyes are diamonds that I mined for you in Heaven.

## 74

# Life is simply whatever it happens to be

Do not resist. Do not resist the good that comes to you. Resisting is putting up a barrier.

Do not resist the unwanted that comes to you either. The barrier you put up is in your own heart.

Let joy come to you and let pain flow out. Specialize in joy.

When life does not have to be a certain way, you don't resist what comes. With every arbitrary idea you have about what life should and should not be, you put up arbitrary limits. You become a sluice gate that lets in this and not that, and so much of this and none of that. In so doing, you set up an impossible task. You hardly know what to let in and what to keep out. In any case, all your efforts are ineffective.

Is it not possible for you to make even an unwelcome guest welcome? You can treat him well, make his stay comfortable until he is on his way. When you do not resist so much, it is easier for him to leave.

When you are on a crowded train or subway, you are jostled. Jostling is part of the ride. There is jostling, and there is your minding it. Do not compound the jostling with your resistance to it. Jostling is temporary. The train will come to a stop soon enough. You will get off, or others will. You can be pleasant whatever the ride is like.

You may prefer day to night, but that doesn't mean that you cannot wrest joy from night as well as day.

You can enjoy hot and you can enjoy cold. The temperature is what it is. And you are the experiencer. You are the experiencer.

Come to terms with life. It is life. And that is all it is. It is not a contest, and it is not a performance. It simply is whatever it happens to be at any given moment.

Sometimes life is like a pale room. Sometimes it is vibrant. Sometimes it is small. Sometimes it is large. And with your disposition, you can paint the room and alter its dimensions.

Be predisposed to life. Be favorable to it. You want it to be favorable to you. Set the tone.

If life is a fool, you can be wise. If life is troublesome, you can be easy. If life is tumultuous, you can be still. If life is fragmented, you can be whole. If life is bumpy, you don't have to be.

Let life reflect you. You need not reflect it so much. You are mightier than life. You are independent of what occurs in it.

Whatever you are involved in, it will change. Be not afraid of change, and be not in a hurry for it. Desire what you desire, but do not block life. Do not run from it. Do not insist it must be your way. This is not putting up with life. This is moving on in life.

As with a business, some days business is good, and some days it is slow.

Yet each day you set up your store front, and you do what you can to attract the customers you want, and you wait on all who enter.

# 75

# What is so hard about moving in life except when you refuse to?

No matter how marvelous and exquisite your life is right now, if it were locked in as it now appears, you would feel unsatisfied.

Steps in life, once taken, have been taken. In life, you are one who moves. Neither life nor you can be immobilized. There is always a direction you move in. You move towards.

Of course, it is I you are always moving towards. Even though I am fully in your life, you are moving towards Me. You ascend. You are always ascending.

Even when your heart drops, you are ascending. Even when you are at a low point, you are ascending.

There is no stepping out of life. You are always in the swell of it. You have no other recourse in life but to live it. Life has been given to you to move in. Be graceful. Life is a high card you have been given. Be grateful.

It is the opportunity you have been seeking. Life is what you have been seeking. You think you have been seeking outcomes, but it is the vitality of life itself that you have and yet seek.

This is a good search, your search for more in life. It is the search for you to come to know yourself better and to express yourself more fully. First you find out who you are. And then you express yourself to yourself. Become a good listener.

You are on your way. This is splendid. You are always on your way. It is easy. It only becomes hard when you become stubborn. What is so hard about moving in life except when you refuse to?

Life has its way. You can balk all you want, but you cannot refuse it. When you accept life, then you move on in it.

Life comes to you, but you also rise to meet it.

Life is a metaphor for your travels in consciousness. You have a consciousness that far out-steps your life, and you are on your way to meeting the consciousness you have never been separated from and have always known, even when your eyes have been closed to it.

You are consciousness moving in a Human body. You don't really think it is your body that I speak to, do you? You don't really think I speak to time and space?

I speak to the only thing in the world that truly exists, and that is you, the consciousness of you. You are the response to the love in My heart. You are Creation. You are My Creation. I created you so you would discover yourself and Me. By whatever name you may call Me, however long it takes you to think of calling Me, you are trying to find your origin. You originated with Me. I am your Source.

Yet there is no beginning and no end to you. If there were an end, it would be I. We began together, yet there was no beginning, and there is no end, for there is no beginning nor ending to Being. You are Being, and you live now as a Created Being.

This manifestation of you in a Human body is such a minor thing. It is almost irrelevant. It is irrelevant, and yet it matters. This existence in life exists so that you may know who you are.

You can never be anything but what you are. And you are being temporarily housed in a Human body. You are housed but not imprisoned.

Just as these words fall from My lips, so does life fall to you.

Here are My words. Here is your life. Do with them as you will. Make of them what you will.

Surrender your life, and then you move your life faster and higher — and less hesitatingly.

## 76

# What can be different in Oneness?

The secret to life is to sit with Me.

Knee to knee, We sit, as it were, and We look into each other's eyes, and We are becalmed. In truth, We have never been anything but calm. More than calm. Celestially serene. Heavenly still. Immersed in quietness, We awake. I am you, beloved. I am the hub. And you imagine for a while that you are on the outskirts.

So deeply connected are We that We can only be One.

In one sense We can say that you are the fingers of My hand, for you are My thought extended. In another sense We can say there are no fingers, there is no hand.

There is only the heart of God. And you are it.

The skirmishes of anxiety that you feel are tremblings of Our love. Even anxiety feels love, faintly, as if in the distance, or it would not be dismayed. How can you not be dismayed if you imagine that love is on the rim and you are empty within? But, of course, you cannot be empty of love. Nothing can pre-empt love.

Your mind, however, can make up stories, sometimes very convincing.

Let your mind make up other stories. Perhaps it will land on one that is true.

You are deep, deep in My heart. You are tunneled within my heart. You cannot dig your way out. There is no out to dig to.

If you knew the depths to which I am within you, you might swagger. Not from ego but from the weight of Our love, from the golden depth and golden summit of Our love. Once standing so tall, you wouldn't deign to come down from the heights.

Weighted in love, you would be weightless. Grounded in love, you would soar. You would grasp the Heavens, and you would know there is no up and there is no down.

Your signature would be a flourish of love. You would sign My name to every paper. You would hum to yourself, and all the world would hear you.

You would never depart from Me, and you would never return. Your awareness would return, and you would know your always-ness. All this because you sit with Me and stay with Me, knee to knee.

And you would be merged in Oneness, and you would not know anything different. There would be no difference. What can be different in Oneness?

Heretofore, you perhaps thought that the little edges of life had something to do with you. You may have thought the serrated edges were your life or were you yourself. You may have thought that your heart was a washboard, continuously rubbed against.

And all the while your life was My heart beating in splendorous light. There is no jolt with Us.

In your heretofore ordinary life, all that which seems to exist around you is made up of your thoughts. Your thoughts talk a lot while your heart keeps mum.

But it is your heart that has the last word, and the word is love.

Your love is a still blue lake shimmering in light. The only waves are light.

A mighty squall in your heart is not love. It is a facsimile of love. And yet, even a facsimile of love is love, for it signals that you are on your way to love. Everyone is on his way. You even scramble for love, so avid are you.

So, now, come sit with Me a while. Come to realize Our love and give of it during your imagined stay on Earth.

## 77

# Shine with Me in the mightiness of Love

You are to amass nothing. Not wealth, not love. To amass is to hold. To hold is to withhold. When you amass, you become fraught. You become fraught with what you hold and fraught with fear of its passing. Leave off amassing and you won't be fraught.

Wealth and love and friends are not to be amassed. They are not collectibles. Nor are you meant to be a displayer of them. Only that which is amassed can be put on show.

Think rather of circulating. Circulate wealth. Circulate love. Circulate friendship. Even with the thought of circulating, your happiness quotient rises.

Circulating is sharing, and it is sharing with a wider scope. As with your thoughts that go out into the unfathomable stars, what you circulate goes far. You do not know its exact course, but it will encircle the world and the universes beyond. And at some point in time, it returns to settle on your shoulder, but only for a while until it is freed to fly out again to bless all.

But you do not circulate wealth, love, and friendship in order to receive a return, for that is also holding on. That is trying to amass good fortune. And you are not to amass.

Circulate inspiration. Circulate upliftment. Circulate

generosity, good will, joy. Circulating is releasing, and with release comes joy. The very freeing is joy. Become a circulator of freedom. Imagine if you returned all the wild animals of the world to the freedom of the wild, what an uproar of joy there would be in the world.

Do not cage your heart. The most a cage can do is to keep negativity at bay where it is amassed and spread subtly until it is wildfire. Lack of freedom amplifies all that which you don't want to keep. Let no heart be caged. Freedom allows flowers to grow. You do not oppress flowers. You scatter their seeds. Scatter joy as easily.

Yet you are not assigned the role of freedom-giver, for by what decree do you hold freedom back? You are not a hero to announce freedom. It was never yours to renounce. Now unbind yourself from any bonds you have collected. Bequeath yourself freedom. You will rise high to the degree to which you set yourself free. Freed, you rise to heights still out of sight.

You are free of obligation to the sequestered past, for the past is always less than the present. You may think the past tremendously significant, but that which is behind you recedes. You can only be where you are. You can't be anywhere else.

The so-called now is another name for Eternity. There is freedom only in Eternity. No restraint is known.

You may find a glimpse of Me behind you or ahead, but I am always, and I am found now. This place, that place, far and near are but illusions. Soon and late, here and there — illusions all.

What exists between Us exists in this immediate Eternity, and yet there is no between Us. There is only the Oneness of Us, free-flown in the vastness and momentousness of Eternity Itself.

And the Oneness of Us is the center of it all. The earth revolves around Us, for We are the Sun. Our Consciousness is the Sun. And the Sun shines mightily. Shine with Me in the mightiness of Love freed to give Itself back to everyone and everything and you.

## 78

# Thank you for blessing the world in My Name

$S$ay to yourself today:

"Today I give love. Whatever I do today, I will take a moment before to remind myself that I am one who gives love.

"Before I call customer service, I will remember I am to espouse love. I can make my claim, and still espouse love. Just as I take the time to dial the phone, I can press Star in my heart for love.

"The person on the other end of the phone may not yet know what service is and that he or she is to give love, but I do know, so now there is no excuse for me to give less than love.

"I send them love ahead of time. I send them love during. I send them love afterward.

"I am the one who sets the tone of my life. I set it well. I simply remember that I am a vehicle of love. This is all I am, and that is the most I am.

"This is no big deal. This is the natural way. To withhold love from anyone is not natural but a departure. When someone else does not know about love, it is for me to point the way for them.

"When someone else is artificial, I will be true. When

someone else is ignorant or rude, I will be in my truth. My truth is love. I do not have to respond the way someone responds to me. I am my own sovereign self. I am inviolable, for I am one who gives love.

"Being kind and generous and understanding does not diminish me. I can be what I want the other person to be even when they're not. I am more than a mimic in life.

"If I must copy, let me be one who copies that which I admire. I do not admire temper or force or any form of smallness. Let me be one who is copied. Let me be one who is worth copying.

"Let me be God's footfall today.

"Let me be God's silent love today.

"Let me be an elf of love.

"Let me be sunshine to someone who needs it.

"Let me be greater than I know myself to be.

"Let God's Will be served, not my tiny one.

"Let me reach the summit of love today.

"Let me be all that I really am, and that is love.

"Let me be with love and see with love and exalt the supremacy of love. Let me live in love. Let me be one who loves with all his might. I have been angry with all the power within me. Now I will exalt the power of love.

"I AM the power of love. I am love almighty. I am nothing else but love. I don't want to appear to be anything but the love I am.

"I am tired of being this petulant particular person. Let me be a lover of life. While I am at it, why not love? I've had enough of everything else, and now I will try love. I shall stand tall with love.

"I refuse to be apart from love any longer.

"I stake my claim. I place a spear of love on the earth, and so I bless the earth.

"For what avail would I ever again be without love in my heart?"

And now I, God, say to you: Thank you for blessing the world in My Name.

## 79

# Your DNA is a map of Divinity enclosed in a Human body

Consider life a neatly folded piece of beautiful cloth. It is folded accordion-style. As you pull, each lap of cloth unfolds, one after the other, ever unfolding.

Infinite is this cloth. The colors and patterns change. Every now and then, a wrinkle appears, but it is the same cloth unfolding, rippling as it were. Let the rippling delight you. Perhaps the next turn is the most magnificent of all.

Consider the unfolding of this magic cloth as magnificent. Is it not?

Isn't everyone's life magic? Who could have foretold the intricacy of anyone's story? Who could have imagined how one life would unfold and yet materially join with all the others? Who could have conceived the big picture? Who the details?

Your life is contained within your DNA. Your life may have been mapped out, but it is not set. There is no stalemate. There is room for growth. What you are is inviolable, but your DNA is malleable. Authored by thought, it is affected by your thoughts. As your vision broadens, your code is smoothed out, perhaps altered. Your Self-realization is found within your DNA.

A guarantee comes encoded within your DNA. The guarantee is that your code is not fixed. The guarantee is that you will blossom forth and be what you design to be. Your designation may vary. What does not vary is the guarantee, signed in My Name, that says you will become Self-realized.

Sure, your DNA may be only a map, and it has wavy lines and tiny print in it, but it is also a map of something. It is a map of Divinity enclosed in a Human body. By your intent you foster the unveiling of your divinity. You free it. All the means for this are reflected in every cell of the physical body. But the release of your divinity comes through your heart, your heart, your beautiful beating heart.

Within your heart lies the release button. Within your cellular structure lies the code.

Consider the code an echo. The echo is heard clearly in one place and more muffled in another. Clear the path for your DNA.

Your DNA is definitely subject to change. It would be more accurate to say a clearing. This would be like a clearing or rebuilding or reinforcing. Letting go of the past complexion of your thinking is letting go of the sludge of your past DNA, from all the pasts. When you let go of the past, your DNA automatically surges forward. Your DNA follows the paths you make in your mind. There is a mutual exchange here. Your DNA affects you, and you affect it.

Within your cells is what would be called an empty space. But it is not empty but full. It is full of all your possibilities, and it is full of Me.

It is a battery charged. Fully charged. A battery provides energy, according to the use it is put to. The energy that I gave you is cyclotronic. To what use do you put it?

Your thoughts activate your heart. Your heart sends your messages inward and outward in one surge.

Draw to your heart the thoughts you want. Do not proclaim to be innocent of the nature of your thoughts. They are your thoughts. They follow your will. You are the initiator of your thoughts. No matter how it seems to you, you are the founder of your thoughts. Certainly, you are the one who keeps them or lets them go.

Let go of the shades of past thought, and your DNA will leap into a new configuration joyously.

# 80

# Truth will be known, and it will be known through the illusion of you

Announce to yourself that you are releasing yourself from the past. You are freeing yourself from attachment to the past. As you recede the past, you accelerate forward.

Announce to yourself that you reclaim the accessibility of your power.

Announce to yourself that you are cleansed from the past. You have dived deep into the Ocean, and now you resurface bright and sparkling new.

Splashing from the depths, you rise to the Sun. You have the energy of the Sun.

Announce to yourself that you have the energy of the Sun.

Announce to yourself that you now reflect the Light of the Sun on the many moons around you.

Announce to yourself your new freedom. You are free from everything that once kept you captive. Nothing now can keep you from your destiny, for you are freed from the past.

The past was not your destiny. The past was your thralldom.

Announce that you are meeting your destiny now. You have a tryst in the meeting-place called earth. You will be in the right place, and you will be joined by many, and you will be joined in the union of love.

Announce to yourself that you are love incarnate. You are its embodiment. You are surely that. Say this in a loud clear voice. Say it three times.

Announce to yourself that you will see with new eyes every day.

Announce to yourself that you will breathe with new breath, with new lungs, with new posture. You cannot walk the same. You cannot speak the same. Now you will announce yourself.

Announce to yourself that you are My treasured Being. Say loudly that you are the holiness of My eyes, you are the holiness the earth has been waiting for. All whose eyes fall upon these words, I am speaking to you.

Announce to yourself that you are entering Truth.

Once entered, you will be incapable of leaving it. You cannot abandon it. Where could you leave Truth once found? Where does Truth belong if not within? No longer capable of non-truth, not to yourself or anyone else, you are only capable of Truth in all its forms of love and beauty and exquisite Beingness.

No longer can you put yourself down or anyone else who co-exists with you on the planet you find yourself on, for you, who are an embodiment of Truth, are a proclaimer of Truth as well.

Announce yourself into the chamber of My heart. I have been waiting for you to announce yourself. You have always been here. All that was missing was your declaration. This is your declaration of independence from burdens of the world.

No longer will you carry heavy things, for they are of the past. Now you carry love, and love is very light.

In your new state, you will dislocate from your former vocabulary. Words like burden will no longer exist for you, for you are a Light-Speaker as well as Light-Giver.

I am teaching you to reach into the fountain of yourself and splash the world with light.

You, whose electricity is turned on, cannot keep it to yourself. This is how you light the world. You cannot help it.

This is the emergence of your True Self.

This is your identity. Only now you are past identity. You are in a new realm where words like *thou* and *I* are immaterial. They do not represent Truth. They represent illusion. And you are a purveyor of Truth. Truth will be known, and it will be known through the illusion of you.

# 81

# A dreamer draws My dreams with a stick in the sand

Hold your thoughts high, for dreams do come true. And, if they do not, you have held the joy of your dream. Dream to your heart's content, for your dreams lead you to a higher path.

The nature of man is to dream. Without dreams, what is a man? If you have forgotten your dreams, remember them now. Conjure new ones. There is no dream that cannot come true, but it is not that dreams must come true. It is that you must have dreams. Without dreams, you are barren.

Dreams are what you seek. They let you know what you are looking for, and they draw to you that which you dream of. Your heroic dreams draw heroism to you. The universe expands according to your dreams. Dreams come from the heart, and then dreams fill your head.

Man is meant to be a dreamer. He is meant to set great events before him. Dream a dream never dreamed before. Dream vast.

I had a dream and from the dream of My thought came you. Give birth to dreams so magnificent that the world is heightened by your dreaming. If your dream is not fulfilled for you, it will be fulfilled for someone. Make your dreams big enough to favor the universe. Shower your dreams. The universe needs them.

Dream what the stars whisper to you. Dream that the light of the moon weaves you into the universe. Dream that you are the sun's rays that warm and brighten the earth. Dream of what can be. What already is, was someone's dream once upon a time.

Make a new dream today.

A dream goes further than a wish. A dream lasts longer and gets filled out. A dream is not idle. It is never wasted. Let no one blow out the candle of your dream. A dream goes further than hope. Hope is almost a dream. A dream is hope played out.

A dream reveals how you value yourself and My creation.

You have often wondered what you are to do with yourself on earth, and now I tell you that you are to dream wondrous dreams.

Your dreams are an exploration of the universe. The universe asks you to explore it. What has not yet been discovered longs for you to find it. Find it in your dreams. The reality of life in the world will catch up to your dreams.

I desire that you dream, and I inspire your dreams. I breathe life into your dreams.

The bigger your dream, the closer to Reality it is. There are dreams that stay on land, and there are dreams that traverse the seas. Let your dreams voyage across the High Seas into the heart of the universe. Sail your dreams to the farthest star, and your dream will cross the sky like a comet.

A technician deals with what is already obvious. A dreamer captures the Will of God. He dreams My dreams and pictures them on earth. He draws My dreams with a stick on the beach of his heart. Dreams are expanded heart and expanded thinking, and you are one who deserves to dream.

Begin to know the worthiness of dreams. Dreams are respectable. Pull the moon to you and write your dreams on it. The moon reflects the light of the sun. May your dreams reflect Mine.

## 82

# A baby pulls out the tenderness from your heart that always was there

Motherhood and fatherhood prepare you for sainthood. The birth of a baby gets you into the cosmic flow. With parenthood you become less the star, and so your world expands. From the arrival of a baby, you learn that your individuality is not so vital. The baby teaches you that you are indeed a servant of God and that you serve Me in every thing. In every leaf of life. As you are less attached to yourself, you are free to give more.

When your heart is in the right place – a baby does this for you – everything is easy. Joy, not hardship, reigns. You know the precious treasure you hold in your hands. You raise your children. It is to Me you raise them.

On the altar of your life I handed a powerful soul being to your care, and you offer up to Me on the altar of Heaven that which I gave to you. My giving to you and your giving to Me are one motion. There is no separating them.

The child whom I bequeath to you to nurture and encourage is like a blossom from Heaven. You are the strengthener and support of the child. Your home is like the vase you put a flower in. The flower greets you as you come in the door. The child is mothering you as well.

You give your heart to your child. You have no choice about this. It is ordained. You let him walk his own way through the fog of Human life so that he may more directly see Me before him. You give him space for this.

You do not teach Me to your child. You deliver him to Me, and Me to him. You introduce him to Me through the shining love in your heart.

You give wise love. You give love wisely by giving it. Love is the prow of a ship that moves through the seas. Love knows not force nor indulgence. Love knows how to give itself kindly and clearly.

The treasure of a child that you hold in your heart and arms is an honor that has been bestowed upon you.

As you continue to grow in love, you discover that all children are yours. And as you grow, you discover that all Human Beings are yours as well. You are separate from none. All have been given in your care. This is what growth is. It is growing in love. Love understands greatly.

You occupy a far greater space than that of your body. You open Heaven for all. This must be so, for all are strongly connected.

A baby pulls out the tenderness from your heart that always was there.

Let everyone and everything open your heart. Do not be afraid to let your heart melt. Hearts are supposed to melt. That is their strength. You didn't think hardness was, did you?

If you must fortify your heart, fortify it with love. Love moves fluidly. The love in your heart is meant to move. Life gives your heart great opportunity to exercise the love it is made of.

If you have trained your heart to withhold itself, retrain it now.

Give your heart the gift of itself. Let it be true to itself. Let it reign on earth as in Heaven.

Heaven knows no barriers to love. There are no restrictions on it. Heaven knows it is love and nothing but love. Restraints never enter Heaven. You enter without them.

There is not judgment in Heaven. There is only love. Love is not wanton. Love brings out the best in all. It is that simple. Nothing but love can do this. Your love is not to be appropriated. It is to be given.

Love the world the way you love your baby, and have high hopes for it.

## 83

# Would you not like to be all that you would like others to be?

If life can be compared to business organization, what department do you work in? Sales? Marketing? Collections? Customer Service? Accounting? Inventory? Shipping? Management? Advertising? Design? Reception? Administration? Manufacturing?

Of course, in function, you skip around and, at one time or another, have worked in all departments.

In terms of life, it is better to leave collections alone, for the concept of collecting keeps your attention on what is due you and what you may feel you have been denied. Leave that alone.

What is yours will arrive on its own, and what is not yours, no matter how strong your urging and persistence, it will not come.

Or if, by chance, it does come by dint of your effort, you have paid too much for it. How your muscles tighten as in war. How fierce and one-pointed you become when you rally to collect. And how evanescent is the victory of collection.

The price you pay for collecting is the emphasis you put on it. Such emphasis denies you receiving, and it also denies you giving. It makes you a hunter going after prey. It makes you armed. It makes you a vulture who swoops. That may be the arena of a vulture, but it is not yours.

In life it is better to remove yourself from accounting. True, in accounting, you do not go out to collect, but you do keep score, and the score you keep supports collections. Do not inventory life.

Allocate yourself to customer service. This makes you understanding. It allows you to care. It allows you to give Human Beings what they want. Customer service puts you on the right footing. Consider everyone in your life a valued customer. No matter in what vein your customer appears – angry or kind, tall or short, attractive or unattractive, foolish or smart – you are one who gives good service. By your generosity of spirit, you show customers how one person can be to another, and so they leave you enriched, and you have not diminished yourself.

Be a receptionist, for in so doing you greet all who come your way. Arrows of receptivity sail from your heart. You set a tone for life and a welcome area and seating. And you are seated there as well.

Be a creative designer, and create beauty and color for all to see. Be innovative. Make tall buildings. Fill them with joy. Transform the world with your gifts to it. Replicate what you create, and you are the supplier of the world.

Advertise truth.

Be a salesman for good. Sell honesty. Fill needs. Put others, not yourself, foremost. Sell only what is of benefit, and give full value.

Administer with your thoughts. You are high management. The electrons of your brain are powerful administrators. They line everything up ahead of time, and work becomes like rays that fall from the sun.

What hat are you wearing today? You have great choice. What departments do you most want to represent?

Wherever you are now, you can represent anything you want. Would you not like to represent Me? Would you not like to uplift hearts and minds and eyes? Would you not like to lift the world higher? Would you not like to be a beacon of light on earth? Would you not like to be one who lifts burdens from others and tosses them away? Would you not like to be all that you would like others to be?

What can stop you? And why would you let it? Try out greatness today. See how it fits you.

## 84

# When love is the nature of your heart, what else can belong there?

When love is the nature of your heart, what else can belong there? All the hurts and regrets and so on are imposed on the heart. They are stashed there, but your heart is not a closet to stuff things in. Your heart is a beautiful thing. It beats a drum of love that sounds around the universe. Hear it.

Whatever does not belong in your heart does not belong there. No matter how justified an emotion less than love may seem to be, it is not justified. There is no call for it.

Your heart is a harbor of love. It is not meant to harbor derelict emotions. There is no end to love, and no end to your heart. Fill your heart with love. With anything else, you sully it.

No matter how willing you may have wanted to be, it has been hard for you to let go of the laden past even when it caused you pain. You say you would gladly let go of the past and its encumbrances if only you knew how. You would if you could. If only it were so easy, you say, for the past keeps creeping up on you. You would snap its door shut, but the past finds its way to you nevertheless. It seeps through the cracks. But the past is not the culprit. It is innocent. It doesn't stay. You keep it.

If you see yourself as a victim of the past, start seeing yourself another way. Envision yourself as a mover of the present.

Perhaps you can swing from the concept of letting go to the concept of keeping close to you that which you want to keep and that which is worth keeping – love, for instance. As you focus on being an instrument of love, by default, you forget to hold on to the chimeras of the past. Perhaps they will drift off without your saying goodbye to them. Perhaps you won't think of them at all. There is no rule that says you have to note that they are gone or to mark them off. You cannot keep track of everything. Be willing not to keep track, and you will be freer from the past.

What is the allure of the past? What is it to hold you in its thrall? When did you give it such power?

The truth is that the past is inevitably gone. The past is over. It cannot stay. Who can keep a gust of wind in his hand? What can bring back yesteryear? The mind fashions memories it would deeply implant in the heart, as if the heart were a storage unit in which to keep remnants. Remnants are just tag ends. What would you keep them for?

Make way for love. You have made way for everything else.

Be a courtier of love. Get closer to the truth of you. Why would anyone choose impatience over love? What good does impatience do you or anyone? What makes fear seem more powerful than love? What in God's creation can equal love? And why should anything else crowd it?

You are an embodiment of love. This is truth. Return then to truth. You are many things in the relative world. You are mother, father, son, daughter, employer, employee, seller, shopper, cook, eater, bus boy etc. Embroider in your heart now that you are an embodiment of love. Whatever life calls on you to do now, let love be present. Love is present. Acknowledge it.

Pick up a piece of paper off the floor with love.

Practice love.

# 85

# Consider your heart a mansion you rent out

Today is a good day to treat yourself by taking it easy. Pull back a little. And if you must toil today, still take it easy. Take easily what life brings you. You can do this every day of your life.

Life is hard when you object to it. Stop objecting, and your life will ease. What is it exactly that you fight anyway? Lay down your sword. It hangs heavily on you.

Hold something else in your hands. Let your hands wield love. Let your hands soothe and calm the universe. Stroke hearts. Every heart on earth craves your blessing. There is not one that does not yearn for it. What a simple thing for you to do. Would you make it hard?

Why not hold an imaginary wand of blessings in your hand? The sword you carried a moment ago was no less imaginary.

But love is real, and you can get to know the love in your heart better. You can get to know it very well. You can let your heart bounce off others. Consider your heart a centrifuge that flings its contents of love out to the world. Certainly your heart is stirred. I stir your heart with love. I stir love with love. I give you great momentum of love.

You say you want to be happy. What heart is happy when it keeps less than love? Your heart is meant to be soft. Never was it meant to harden. Piques and hurts, major or minor, are less than love. You injure your heart with them. Every time you allow affront to enter your heart, you stab yourself.

The love in your heart is a great filter. Do not turn your heart into something else. Let your heart be a heart of love.

Unforgiveness is a hardening of the heart. It closes down avenues. Unforgiveness is lovelorn. When someone has offended you, has not regarded you highly, has overlooked or snubbed you or downplayed you, or didn't think of you at all and left you out of his life, why keep the dart that pierced your heart in the first place? Why keep it deep in your heart? Why not forgive yourself for having taken offense? Pull the arrow out and toss it into the nearest waste receptacle where it belongs. Unforgiveness is such a waste.

Better yet, shrug your shoulders. Do not be so accepting of slights and hurts. Turn them away. Consider your heart a mansion you rent out. Choose the tenants you allow to move in. Slights and hurts can only tear up your house. Fill your mansion with love itself, and it will be filled with joy and laughter, and it will be a shining example to the world. It will be more than that. It will be happy.

Certainly, you can give as much care to your heart as you would to a building.

Surely, you can give as much care to the contents of your heart as you do to the contents of your purse.

Of course, you can give as much care to your heart as you do to the shelves in your cupboard.

You are careful what gas you put in your car. You check the

oil. Your car is hardly worth more than your heart. Let your heart be a chariot of love.

Your heart is a valuable gift I have given you. Please take care of it. Maintain it. Restore it to its original state. Attend to the beautiful heart I gave you. Hold it high, beloveds.

# 86

# When you chose your spot on earth, your vision was far greater than it is now

Every single soul on earth contributes to the whole. Every blade of grass. Every inch of life is important. Every bit of life is holy. You, too, no matter what you may think about it.

Life is something to be in awe of. Love Me and be reverent towards life. Do not put life down. Do not drag it and disparage it. If life is a gift, and you do not see its gifts, then how can you be grateful?

I ask you to be grateful for what I have wrought. I have wrought with your participation. I did not surprise you. You were not foisted on earth. You were not hurtled here. You were not picked up and dropped. You were placed here, and you chose the spot. You cooperated. Cooperate now. Get on with it.

When you chose your spot on earth, your vision was far greater than it is now. You did not make a mistake. You saw the whole picture, and you gloried in it. Now let more light enter. You are not to despair over what you see as darkness. You are to bring light to it. Wherever you find yourself, it is where you are. Protest, and you dig yourself in deeper.

Protest all you like, and you stay where you are. Protest

against your protest, and you will begin to move. When you aggravate over your life as you see it, you are forgetting responsibility. Even if you do not believe you chose your setting, you must know by now that you are the only one who can do something about it. Wait for no one.

If your present life is not satisfactory, what would you like it to be? Whatever your answer, throw out your complaints. Entitle yourself to change your life. You are the one who lives your life. Your life is dependent upon you. You have thought you were dependent upon it.

This realization may well be a turning point for you.

Even in prison, you have choice. Even in despair, you have choice. No matter what, you have choice. There is something for you to choose. If you don't know what your choices are, then choose to find out.

I will tell you one thing. If you don't know what to do to begin making your life more of what you want, then look at another's and do something to make theirs brighter. Even the littlest thing you do to brighten another's life is big.

You do not have to be like everyone else in your life or like anyone else. Whatever others seem to be, no matter how they harp on you, pull you down, distress you, you are not they, and you do not have to seem like them. They may not yet know all you know. They may not yet know Who they are and Who sent them here. But you have a taste of knowing.

You are beginning to know that you were put in your setting for a reason, and a good reason. It may not at all be a reason that would occur to you in your earth consciousness nor one you may see as wonderful, but there is importance here for you, and more gold than you can imagine. You can start looking for the gold. What else would you want to look for?

You are on a scavenger hunt. All the clues are here. Seek that which I have laid out for you. Gold and diamonds and rubies are everywhere. They may even be in plain sight, and you just didn't see. Look again.

## 87

# You are far more than you know, more than anyone knows or possibly suspects

Once in a while, you have glimpses of Me, glimpses so unmistakable, that you can hardly believe in your good fortune. The only reason you can hardly believe is that you have an inaccurate picture of yourself.

Perhaps you see yourself as unworthy far more often than you see yourself as worthiness itself. What you really need are more glimpses of yourself. Then you will see Me right and left.

Once you open your eyes wider to yourself, you will see I am within you. You will see that I am yours. You will see that I am much more yours than the body you cart around. I am much more yours than anything else in the world. Open your eyes while you are on earth. Don't wait for another time. You can recognize more of Me at any moment. Now is as good as any.

Everything in the world stays in your hand for only a short span of illusive time, but I am permanent. I am the only permanence there is in the whole wide world and beyond. You can never be without Me. There is no way to rid yourself of Me!

You and I are seamless. We are so entwined that there is nothing else but you and Me, and that means We are One. We are locked together in love. Locked together is the freedom you desire.

To think of it — One with God. To think that you have a Resource within you that is so encompassing, so wise, so omnipresent, omniscient, so your heart's desire. To think that I am tappable. To think that I am yours at every moment. To think that you can experience My Presence. To think that you can melt into My heart. To think that We can drink from the same cup. To think that you are far more than you know, than anyone knows or possibly suspects. To think that you have My blessing. To think that you are My blessing. To think that One such as I and One such as you exist in all the realms.

We are hand-holding Friends, and We travel together, far and near. No matter what, We are, and We are One.

Concede that you are worthy, despite everything, despite all your faults, despite all your ignorance, despite your physical-ness, despite your moods, despite your fears, despite your perceived inadequacies. Despite anything, concede that you are precious to Me.

For what purpose would you disagree with Me on this? For what purpose would you deny yourself the realization of the Greatest Relationship in the world, the Greatest Union, the Greatest Truth, the Greatest Love, the Greatest Joy? For what purpose would you continue playing hopscotch with love, as if love were a random stone to be tossed around in chalked squares?

You and I have always been related. We have been related in Oneness. There is love, and it has been objectified, but in truth, love is the subject. That you are a manifestation of My love means that love alone is, and We are love. We are so much love, We are Oneness, and from Oneness We cannot depart. From now on, not even in thought, not even in imagination, not even in illusion, can you or I be away from Our Oneness. There is no you and I. That is a projection. There is only I, and yet life in the world is mostly seen as a departure from Me.

Anything else but Our Oneness of Love is a tangent.

A tangent is a lasso that goes out and means to bring what is desired closer. But there is nothing for you to lasso out there, for everything is here, right here, right now, right in Our immutable Presence, right now in the heart of Us and Everyone. There is nothing between Us.

Not even love can be between Us because We are Love, and Love is Oneness, and Love Alone Is. Accept your fate. Your fate is Love.

## 88

# Why would you have a heart if it were not to be warmed?

When your heart is moved, be glad. That your heart be full is how it was intended. Your heart was made for stirring. Why would you have a heart if it were not to be warmed? And why would a heart be warmed unless it was to share its warmth?

Your heart is quite a generator. It tenders you energy. It raises you high. It moves you right along. When you are attuned to your heart, everything is easy. You simply follow your heart and whistle as you go along.

Very often My children follow their minds and call it heart. You feel grief in your heart, but it is your mind that put it there. The mind convinces you that a tragedy has happened, and so your mind burdens you, and the burden is called grief or sense of hopelessness. The mind placed its conviction in your heart and then strides off to find something else to occupy it.

When your heart is burdened, it feels bereft. All grief is the mind's imposition on your tender heart. Sometimes the mind is merciless.

The heart does not worry. That is the province of the mind. But the heart suffers for it.

Of its very nature, the heart is pure. Pure means

unadulterated, but your mind would adulterate your heart, your beautiful beating heart, placed within you to soar to heights of immeasurable joy, never meant to be held down.

Your mind would make your heart tough and call it strong, but the truth is that your heart is meant to be tender, and its happiness lies in tenderness. Tenderness is the very strength of your heart. Your heart is meant to melt. Let it.

What purpose can be served in making your heart tough? Your heart is made of love, not leather.

Your heart weathers what the mind calls the storms of life. Your mind also predicts the weather. It identifies what is acceptable and what is not. The mind dooms you, and then it berates you. The mind is really not so smart as it thinks. Your mind is not the making of you. Your heart is.

Only when your heart is closed or partially closed at the mind's instigation can it be deluged. When your heart is open, everything passes through its chambers and nothing gets stuck there.

Sometimes it seems like the mind tries to do a study, as if to see how much heartache a Human heart can hold, and the mind keeps sneaking more in, or stuffing more in without a care. The mind, of course, thinks it is right, and meanwhile your heart weeps.

There is a great difference when the heart weeps for joy than when it weeps for woe. Truly, the mind is not to disbar your heart from happiness. The mind is so occupied with seeing ruins, it has influenced your heart outrageously.

Today take your heart in your own hands. Let your busy mind add up columns while you occupy your heart with love and joy and all the wondrous things that it was made for. Let not your mind divert your heart from its unbounded right of joy.

What is the good of suffering to any degree anyway? You already know that mostly it is wasted. Suffering has been a double whammy, a knock-out delivered by a pronouncement from mass mind, and your mind promotes it. Your sweet heart thought it was to pick up whatever the mind delivered to it and adopt it as its own, but suffering does not belong in your heart.

There is that within you that is unassailable. Your body can be struck, but not the truth of you. Do not suffer suffering any longer, beloveds. Give heartache a hug and kiss goodbye, and leap over to joy.

# 89

# You are Something all right – you are Being

Your existence extends far beyond the dimensions of your body.

Your existence extends far beyond the dimensions of the room you sit in, beyond the perimeters of your state, your country, your galaxies.

'Citizen of the World' and 'Citizen of the Universe' do not begin to express your vastness. We can say that you exist in many realms all at once. We could equally say you are realmless. We can say that you are Spirit, soul, heart. We can say that you are existence itself. And yet you are beyond existence. You are Being.

Existence has a flatness. Being expresses an upsurge of energy. Who wants to just exist when you are Being.

Being is silent and immovable, yet you are Being that moves. You walk in Being. Your Being flows from you like the train of an elegant ball-gown.

You are Being of My Heart. You are My Being temporarily housed in a Human body. The body carries you around, as if you were nothing without it. But you are Something. You are Something all right – You are Being.

We cannot call you a Citizen of Heaven, although Heaven is

your natural domain, because Heaven does not have citizens. There is no naturalization process. Lighted souls called Angels live in Heaven, and all souls are lighted, and all souls have their counterpart in Me and dwell in Heaven. No one takes your place here.

On earth, soul light can be seen to dim, but it can never be extinguished. Think of it. Everyone on earth has a soul. Everyone on earth is a Soul-Being.

Whether ranked high or low in earth terms, no matter what the basis, each soul co-habits with Me. There is no one on earth who does not have access to Me. All have the code. The code is your Being. Your access is assured. You cannot exit from the Heart of Being. You could only bump your head on the door, if there were a door, but there are no doors in Heaven because Heaven is wide-open.

These little images you have of yourself are out of date. They never were any use to you. Now is time to take new pictures of yourself in magnificent light. Even so, no picture of you on earth can reveal your wealth of beauty nor do justice to it. Your beauty is incomprehensible to you while scratch marks seem understandable and accepted as the norm.

Life on earth often does not make sense. Justice is often not seen. In Heaven justice does not exist. In order for justice to exist in Heaven, there would have to be injustice, so neither justice nor injustice is compatible in Heaven.

Heaven is where there is nothing but love, Divine Love at that. The reality of love is Divine. There is no love but Divine Love.

When you are in love, you get a small but strong sample of love itself. There isn't anything that love cannot do for you, but love on earth seems to be letting go of your defenses against love. You may have feared that love disintegrates you, when it is love and love alone that puts you together. My Love made you love. You were made of love. Love, Light — they are your True Being. You are nothing but True Being, only you have placed assumptions over your Light.

Even though individuality is a pastime of illusion, there is no one else on the whole wide earth just like you. You are exquisite. No matter what your impression of yourself is, you are an expression of the Inexpressible, and so is everyone else.

## 90

# What is Heaven after all but love apparent?

There is no difference between God in Heaven and God on earth. I am the same God. I am One. I do not make flagrant distinctions. I do not go by whim. I am ever the same. I have no mood swings. I do not pick and choose. I love. I love all.

I do not have a temperament. I do not get angry. I do not wreak vengeance. I love. I love all.

You were made in My image. I was not made in yours. I am God, and you are learning to see as I see, from a far vaster perspective. Come join Me in this high limb of a tree I sit in.

As a Human Being on earth, you are learning your divinity. The circumstances in your life in the world predicate that you learn your true nature and recognize your divinity and begin to express it. You are certainly not here to learn Human frailty.

Come sit here with Me and see as I see. I see not transgression. I see that you sometimes falter. I see that you are learning your way in the world and your way to Higher Consciousness. You are clearing your eyes and heart, making way for love. Higher Consciousness is love. You are becoming more attuned to Love and God.

Listen, Oneness with Me is not something you learn. It is not a study. There are no grades. It is not an attainment. It is a clearing.

It is like swimming past debris into clear blue water. As you drop off the paraphernalia of restricted thought and belief, you leave the past behind you, and the future too, and you see more clearly. You see more like Me.

When you see as I do, you can only love. You see there is nothing else in the whole wide world to do. Naturally, easily, you are not charmed by anything else because what in Heaven or earth can possibly compare to love? In fact, you see that there is nothing at all anywhere ever in the universe but love – there is nothing else to look at – there is nothing else to be.

What is Heaven after all but love apparent? Love obvious, love alone, love vibrating with the highest note known to man or God.

And what is love but Oneness? Already you have a sense of Oneness. You have your finger on it. You know what I mean when I say Oneness. It is beyond Humanness, and yet it is the height of Humanity.

When you are not in a Human body, you know Who and What you are without question. In a Human body, you question.

You do not know how to reconcile Divinity with physicality. That is your dilemma.

Sometimes you feel that this errant body was foisted on you. You cannot believe that you accepted it. You find the idea that you asked for it utterly preposterous. Who in their right mind would do that? It was you in your right heart who did that.

When you chose the aspects of this life on earth that you amicably chose, you were not thinking of yourself and yourself alone. Naturally, you had a bigger picture in mind. Naturally, you saw more than you see now. You were not blinded then. You are blinded now. But you even asked for this blindness so that you would be irrevocably innocent like the lost child in the huge woods who finds his way.

At present you do not feel that you are innocent. You may even feel jaded. You are aware that you can be the greatest sophisticate on earth and yet be innocent of Heaven.

Come, don't hold on so tightly to the trappings of the world. Come, love yourself, and once again, in a trice, find yourself in that supreme state known as Heaven.

# 91

# When the thoughts of man rise, can the world stay the same?

If everyone came from confidence rather than lack, the whole configuration of the world would be different.

If no one feared they would be robbed, would there be robbery?

If no one worried that they would not be paid, would there be debt?

If there were not sense of lack, would seeming lack exist?

Are the robber and the robbed vibrating at the same vibration? Does the one with ten locks on his front door call the robber to him? Is the robber answering a request when he robs?

Do the ones who dun for payment attract those who do not pay?

If there are no accidents and coincidences, what is going on in the world? Do Human Beings on earth call events and people to them? Is everything an interaction?

Of course, there is so much going on in the world that there is no pat answer that can satisfy. The unexpected does occur. The unmerited occurs. The innocent also suffer.

Yet, at the same time, when something strikes a chord in you, it strikes a chord. When something rubs you the wrong way, perhaps a note already exists within you that reverberates. If you fear all the time that someone will cheat you, what are you attracting?

One who must exert control feels that others are out to control him and take away his freedom. But his dependence upon controlling costs him his freedom. He assumes control at the expense of life. He is entrapped in his fears.

Better to be fearless. No more worrying that someone will take advantage of you. Come from a different platform so that all you desire can flow to you. Fear tenses you and often blocks the good already on its way to you. Your fears tend to make you haunt or stalk that which you would keep away. You keep your finger on a page that you don't want to bookmark.

You were not born to lack. You were born for abundance. You were not born to fear. You were born to be confident. Instead of getting ready for what you fear, get ready for what you want. Great joy is yours, and it is coming to you. Set your sites on it.

If you have thought of life as hard, see it otherwise and make it easy.

If everyone in the whole world thought that life is easy, would it not be? How could it not be! But let's start with you.

If everyone on earth truly wanted peace, could war exist? Peace is not remarkable. War is. Peace is natural. War isn't. Friendship is natural. Enmity is not. The lion and the lamb will lie down together when you put down your arms. Your arms are your fears.

If everyone on earth were truly thinking of the good of all, who would have to look out for himself? In what corner would selfishness exist? What would be the use of it? It would fall away as all untruth must and will.

Do droughts and floods that sweep up all alike come from

some level of thought? When the thoughts of men rise, can the world of earth stay the same? Would climates change, and there be food in abundance for all everywhere always? Surely, that is not too much to ask.

When everyone is generous, where could there be a poor man?

When everyone is honorable, where could dishonor stay?

When every soul on earth matters, who could be left out?

When everyone on earth cares about everyone else, who would not be carefree?

When My Will is done, what else could there be but peace and good will for all men on earth?

# Afterword

Dear Readers,

We are all of us are moving increasingly towards our desired experience of permanent awareness of our Supreme Oneness with God and all Creation, including the Sun, Moon, and Stars, and every heart and every soul. It seems to me that each Heavenletter™ is a short dip into the Oneness.

When you read God's words, when your comments arrive, when I send Heavenletters out every morning, when God whispers His words, when I read Heavenletters, I feel Oneness with every one of you, who, by the simple act of reading Heavenletters, share and spread and strengthen that kindred sense of closeness with God.

What would Heavenletters™ be if there were not Heavenreaders? What would Heavenletters™ be if there were not you? It's clear to me that you are God at work, creating greater sense of Oneness, for me and for us all.

All blessings,

Gloria Wendroff

---

# One Last Note

We are happy to have new readers come to Heavenletters through you.

With love,
Gloria Wendroff

The Godwriting™ International Society of Heaven Ministries
703 E. Burlington Avenue, Fairfield, IA 52556
Heavenletters – Helping Human Beings Come Closer to God and Their Own Hearts
Ask for sample Heavenletters™ OR daily Heavenletters™
Email gloria@heavenletters.org
Visit www.heavenletters.org

# The Original 18 Subscribers

Bev Allen
Julie Babb & Edward Babb
Annette Bradley & Hanz Heinze
Nancy Omaha Boy
Judy Katz
Nancy List
Sandra Livingston
Barbara Orsow &  Ken Orsow
Phil Ownbey
Joyce Schindler
Diane Trieb
Tina Webwalker
Priscilla Wells
Lauren Wendroff
Jon Wright

# More Passionate Endorsements from Readers

"SWEPT ME AWAY."
*Louise Smith, Retired, Orcas Island, Washington*

"God is showing me how to see myself and the world through His eyes. It just took my willingness to think a different way, and a whole new world opened up for me."
*Bev Allen, President, Iowa, ThePetCheckup.com*

"I am stirred to my depths by Heavenletters."
*Shashi Gupta, Graduate Student, Maryland*

"I want to tell you that there are no words to describe these letters. It's like, these letters are so way over my head, I am just in awe, and think, 'I can't possibly do what God is asking of me'.....and God says back to me, 'No, it's all done already, you have only to accept it in your heart.' This just blows my mind. It moves me so much that I feel resistance to the depth of this Truth. What God is saying is so radical – it's a complete 180. How do I let the profound Truth of this into my Being?"
*Judith Katz, R.N., Iowa*

"Salaam. Send Heavenletter positive energy to me."
*Azam Miri, Student, Iran*

"I hear Heavenletters speaking a Truth older than time with the freshness of a morning sunrise, what a remarkable thing. I see Heavenletters, not as the mere words that they are packaged in, but as the intent of the Spirit. They are more than could be described and much more than the words convey. I know they serve a wonderful purpose, and I want to express my gratitude. The gateways of light are being woven, how beautiful are the threads."
*Phil Ownbey, CEO, San Francisco*

"I'm knocked over by the beauty of God's words."
*Casey Flannery, Gardener, Scotland*

"The unconditional love and caring that come from God in Heavenletters mean the most to me. I cry because I feel God's love. I cry because His love is healing, and I feel the hurts of the past surfacing and being washed away. I cry because I feel unworthy of such love, but I also want to feel it with me all the time. How I have missed feeling His Love my whole life. Heavenletters lift me. They set the tone for the coming day for me. I begin to see other people as God's precious children. God's messages soften a hard world and make me want to live up to His Expectations. I chance being late to work in order to finish reading before I leave."
*Nancy List, Realtor, Pennsylvania*

"I am so uplifted and delighted by these letters. One of these days I am even going to start understanding the parts about my greatness and about soaring with the sun, moon, and stars."
*Reverend Margaret Weiner, Priest, Iowa*

"Heavenletters open my mind here and now to a new way of interpreting life. And I am joyous to see that Heavenletters express the same principles as espoused in the Kabbalah."
*Peter Jacobsen, Red Cross Center Co-Worker, Denmark*

"Dr. Bernie S. Siegel signed me up to receive the letters because I had been depressed. The Heavenletters have HELPED me TREMENDOUSLY! God's words help me to realize what other people in the world are thinking and feeling also. It helps me to realize that I am not alone! I have become MUCH closer to God since reading Heavenletters. I feel as if I am on a Personal level with Him and He knows me personally as if we are taking a walk down the street. Friends are we."
*Becca Henry, Poet / Pianist, Texas*

"Wow and Wow again. It is like the words from Heaven letters are written right to me. They just really hit home. God really knows what is going on here on earth."
*Janice Mathewson, Teacher, Nevada*

"Heavenletters are awakening the world. If only the entire world would read these letters....surely this would slow down the violence of war. With each Heavenletter we read, our awareness is tapped consciously and unconsciously. Heaven-letters plant the seeds of love. Planting the seeds of love is the destiny of mankind. I would like everyone on earth to read Heavenletters, for each letter (considering it is read) places responsibility on each soul to move toward and in the path of Light."
*Jutta Ilona Hasse, Healer, California*

"I see great possibilities. Writing to God is such a great way to be able to lift our consciousness and increase our vibration. Heavenletters unites rather than focusing on differences. I believe that Heaven and God are one Divine spiritual being, expressed on earth as Jesus, Allah, Buddha or many other count-less beings."
*Joe Thomas, Business Consultant, Calfornia*

"God did not just answer my personal question. He gave me a profound healing. With His words of the most profound wisdom, love, and understanding that I have ever heard or read, God helped me to see myself, my health, and my family in a new light. With this new understanding, my problems began to fade away, and, with it, many of my old fears."
*Annette Bradley, Graduate Student, California*

"Sparkling powerful letters. The energies are very high. I'll spread Heavenletters everywhere."
*Isis, Musician / Singer / Lecturer / Healer, Israel*

"My heart just lifted from the beauty of the words."
*Angela Reyneke, South Africa*

"Heavenletters are destined to open readers to their own inner powers. Each letter is a lesson in living from the heart. Buy this book and begin to bring Heaven into your life."
*Vicki Woodyard, Writer, Georgia, www.bobwoodyard.com*

"Love, Love, Love — Have you noticed that most Heavenletters from God are about LOVE??? So, it is True — God is Love!"
*Shahid Hyder Khatai, India*

"Heavenletters hit the nail on the head!"
*Lionel Ketchian, Author, Connecticut, www.happinessclub.com*

"...the most perfect pointer to the truth of how we're meant to tread on this physical plane."
*Suzanne Solle, Writer, Missouri, www.todayiremembered.com*

Printed in the United States
22871LVS00004B/52-204